AN OVERVIEW OF

WHY ISRAEL MATTERS

LEE CUMMINGS

Published by
Radiant Church
8157 E De Avenue
Richland, MI 49083

ISBN: 979-8-9884196-8-6 (paperback)

ISBN: 979-8-9884196-9-3 (e-book)

I dedicate this book to the Dinner Club—Larry and Deb Bauss,
Sharon and especially David Klein.
Your friendship and encouragement have been a gift from God
to Jane and me over the last several years.
I am grateful for the conversations and
the courageous faith of my closest Messianic friend.
Until all Israel is saved!

CONTENTS

1

WHY ISRAEL MATTERS TO ME

Anyone who dares to write a book about Israel better have a good reason to do so, have some skin in the game, or better yet, be thick-skinned. Why? Because as a topic, a country, a land, a people—Israel is controversial. Anything someone writes about Israel, therefore, can provoke intense emotions, including rage that even begets violence. We're seeing this around the world today. Sadly, this is nothing new. That's why I was prayerful and circumspect about writing *An Overview of Why Israel Matters*. I didn't want to simply add more fuel to the ongoing firestorm blazing across the globe. In the end, as you can see I chose to write this book, and I'll explain why momentarily.

But first, I want to do what I saw other authors do in their books on Israel. I discovered in my research that the first pages of their books detail more than their names, publication information, and relevant affiliations. Apparently, authors of these books felt the need to identify their race or religion, their "why behind the what," and their bias right at the beginning of their respective books. I think that's due to how prone to provocation any discussion of Israel is. The thinking behind this probably is what we all think when we go through a TSA PreCheck® before we can get on a flight. Might as well take out all the change from our pockets, remove our belts and shoes, and place all items on the X-ray belt for screening because, in the end, the TSA agent is going to find out what we're carrying on us anyway. Rather than leave you, my reader, guessing what I'm bringing with me and sharing with you on this "flight," how about I just do what my fellow authors did in their books on Israel and tell you the pertinent information here at the beginning.

In the spirit of full disclosure, then, and thanks to a 23andMe® DNA test, I'm 3 percent **Ashkenazi** Jewish (pretty unimpressive, I know, especially to rabbinical genealogists). As for the Indigenous American ancestry I thought I possessed, well, let's just say that DNA doesn't lie but maybe someone in my family liked to tell tales.

Regarding religion, I'm a born-again, Spirit-filled Christian. And I'm a pastor. I've been both for a few decades now.

When it comes to any bias, I'll say it plainly: I'm pro-Israel and pro-Bible, and I believe the Church should be both, too. I'll unpack that a bit throughout the course of this book. Hopefully, my directness won't be off-putting, and you'll give the book a full reading if only to discover just how "pro" I am.

Lastly, as far as the why behind the what is concerned, I guess I should answer that by responding to the following questions:

- When did I become interested in Israel?
- Why did I write this book?

Discovering the Bible Is Israel-Centric

I have always loved the Bible. Going all the way back to my childhood, I remember watching my paternal grandmother and grandfather read the Scriptures, and then I watched them live what they read. Their example marked my life for eternity.

My mother and I lived on and off in my grandparents' home during my first seven years of life. My grandfather got up early each morning, sat in his chair, and read the Bible. Often, I would climb up onto his lap so that he could read it to me. His voice and the content of what he read ignited a fascination with God's Word that is still with me today.

As I got older, I became more inquisitive and would drill my grandparents with questions regarding what the Bible had to say about all kinds of things. One of the subjects that I found especially intriguing was eschatology or end-time prophecy. Whenever I heard my grandparents discuss Bible prophecy, I stopped whatever I was doing and listened attentively to every word they said. I'm not exactly sure why the subject of the end times interested me so much then. Perhaps it had to do with my wanting to understand what was going to happen in the future, or maybe it was the influence of my grandparents' unflagging interest in the end times themselves. No matter its reason or source, I do know that the subject awakened faith in my heart.

After I turned twelve, I had a life-changing encounter with God that shifted the trajectory of my future. That saving and calling event fired up a passion inside me to know the Bible, because I wanted to know *everything* I could about Jesus. This resulted in my spending hours studying the Scriptures. I mean, I consumed the Book! And something profound happened as I studied and grew in my relationship with Jesus. My heart turned kindly and compassionately toward the nation and people of Israel. The Bible, it seemed to me, was all about Israel, from beginning to end. All the stories, the patriarchs, the battles, and the promises centered around this people and this place. I had also heard my grandfather and our pastor frequently talk about 1948 with *the restoration of Israel to the Land as the seminal prophetic event in modern history.* I was captivated not only by Israel's history, but also by the promises that remained regarding her future and how she was centerstage in Bible prophecy.

God began something in those formative years that I simply didn't fully understand at the time. It wasn't until many years later that I discovered He was doing a work in my heart regarding Israel and Bible prophecy. He was knitting them together within me just as the two were knit together in His Word, in history, and in the future.

Turning Hearts toward the Nation and Her People

Many years have passed since my youth, and I have now taught the Bible for over thirty years. As a pastor, I admit that I have not swerved from my convictions regarding the importance and significance of Israel, but as often happens, the immediacy of preaching life application to grow and mature those I shepherd affected how often I preached and what I preached about the subject. Most of the time when I spoke about Israel, I used the nation as an example from the past to teach people about how to live in our American "now." This changed for me, however, in 2018 while I was on a trip to Israel.

Standing in Jerusalem with a tour group and listening to our guide teach about the promises God made to Abraham as an everlasting covenant, loudspeakers from several different directions began to belt out the Muslim call to prayer in Arabic. It was an eerie moment as I could sense the spiritual warfare taking place over this city that God, long ago, marked out as His.[1] Amid the chaotic sounds surrounding me, I remember having an "aha!" moment right then and there, suddenly understanding that there truly is something significant about the Land of Israel, her people, the covenants, and the promises connected to her—that the prophetic oracles spoken thousands of years ago by the prophets are still in play. Furthermore, being alive in proximity to the time that Israel became a nation again after her people had been dispersed among the nations for centuries set anchor into the depths of my heart like it never had before. All at once, I possessed a surety deep in my heart of the urgency of the hour, the prophetic importance of the days in which I was living, and the inseparable and glorious futures of Israel and the Church. This forever changed my perspective and priority.

Since that time, I have returned to studying the mystery of Israel, and I have become a fervent intercessor for the Jewish people. *I believe that, in these last days, God is going to raise up a gentile Church who loves and supports the Jewish people, provoking them unto jealousy in a way that tears down the wall of dullness from their hearts and removes the scales from their eyes.* I have embraced this call as my own and have committed my life and ministry to help restore the heart of the Church back toward the Land of Promise and the People of Promise—toward the City of the great King and, ultimately, the King of kings. *That's why Israel matters to me.* It's also why I wrote this book.

Because Israel Matters

Friend, Israel matters, and I believe Israel matters (1) today, (2) historically, (3) politically, (4) theologically, and (5) to the Church. In the following pages, I present a brief case for each of these reasons, answering some of the most asked questions about issues related to the nation and people. To assist you in getting a better grasp of all things related to Israel, I include a few chronology tables, a glossary,* some recommended resources, and a quick reference Q&A.

By no means is this book meant to be an exhaustive discussion on the topic of Israel and her significance. My goal in writing a shorter work is to provide an overview on the subject, covering the basics in a brief read. It's about making the topic accessible to every believer and utilizable as a tool for instruction and reference.

I pray that, as you read and consider my argument for *why Israel matters*, it will not only inform you, but also awaken within you a heart for Israel and the Jewish people. May you join me in being one of many who stands on the wall of intercession before God until He makes Jerusalem a praise in all the earth![2]

---

* Words in **bold** throughout the text (except for words in headings and subheadings) may be found in the glossary on page 85 in the paperback edition. In the e-book edition, the bold words are linked to the glossary. Definitions are provided there to assist the reader's understanding of the use of these words within this book.

2

WHY ISRAEL MATTERS TODAY

In October of 2023, I planned to preach a series of messages at my church, Radiant Church, in Kalamazoo, Michigan. I thought the series would take us through that month and into the next. Then something happened that changed everything: October 7, 2023.

Immediately, I pivoted and told my ministerial team that, instead, I was going to preach a series titled "Israel, Iran, and the Rising Storm."* Over the course of the next six weeks, I delivered some of what I believe have been the most important sermons I've preached to date. In fact, those messages were viewed tens of thousands of times, and I was interviewed by major media outlets, not because I was an expert, but because I was the rare exception—I was a pastor talking about the events of October 7.

---

* This sermon series is available online on the @RadiantChurch YouTube channel. Here is the web address for the first message: https://www.youtube.com/watch?v=c70ORmWDPy8/. Another message titled "Why Israel Matters" is available at https://www.youtube.com/watch?v=D-3xXrOz3ZA.

In this chapter, we're going to see how October 7 supports the fact that *Israel matters today.* We'll answer the following questions:

- What happened on October 7, 2023?
- How did the world and the Church respond?
- What has been the fallout?

A Day That Will Not Be Forgotten

It could be argued that the global conversation forever changed on October 7, 2023. As Israeli Prime Minister **Benjamin Netanyahu** told a joint meeting of the United States (US) Congress, "October 7 is a day that will live in infamy," likening it to December 7, 1941, and September 11, 2001.[1] On October 7, **Hamas**, a terrorist organization that years earlier gained control over the Palestinian territory of **Gaza**, attacked Israel from all directions and murdered over 1,200 Israelis, most of whom were Jews.[2] Hamas, which in Hebrew means *violence*, took over 200 innocent men, women, and children as hostages.[3] They raped women, murdered entire families, including innocent children and babies, and even filmed their savagery, livestreaming it on social media while celebrating their "victory" over the Jewish nation. This day recorded the greatest loss of Jewish lives since the **Holocaust** in Europe during World War 2.[4]

Within hours, the entire world was watching in real time the full effects of **antisemitism**, Jew hatred, that prior to that moment many doubted could still exist. Compassion and grief were the overwhelming emotions that were experienced by many as they saw the horrors and devastation. People were trying to process how human beings could treat other human beings so brutally. How could members of Hamas look into the eyes of women and children and murder them in cold blood simply because they were Jewish? It was too horrifying and overwhelming for our twenty-first-century sensibilities to take in, let alone understand.

The World Responds

In the coming days and months as Israel responded with force, deploying the **Israel Defense Forces (IDF)** with boots on the ground and airstrikes, the expected response from the international community was that of support and solidarity, much like how the global community stood with the US after the terrorist attacks on 9/11. While many did stand with the nation of Israel in her response, protests began to break out across major cities in the West. Palestinian flags were being waved, accompanied by chants of *"From the river to the sea, Palestine shall be free!"* by almost 100,000 supporters of the Palestinian people—and this was happening on London streets from "Hyde Park Corner, Piccadilly and Trafalgar Square to ... Whitehall and ... Parliament Square."[5] What protestors were chanting was a call for the removal and anni-hilation of the nearly 10 million Jews currently living in Israel.[6] Similar protests were repeated across Europe in major cities such as Madrid, Berlin, Paris, and Amsterdam.

Additionally, open antisemitism at universities across America was manifested as thousands of activists and students took over campuses and refused to allow Jewish students and faculty to enter buildings and classrooms.[7] Scenes of highly agitated activists holding signs with antisemitic tropes, openly attacking Jewish students and faculty, flooded the news and social media. Universities like Columbia in New York City told Jewish students that they should stay home, because the universities could not ensure their safety. The University of Southern California (USC) cancelled its main graduation ceremony due to the protests on its campus.[8] The insanity was overwhelming. And as if it could not become any more surreal, the Security Council of the United Nations (UN) was unable to gather a consensus to issue a condemnation of the actions of Hamas.[9] But in the coming months, the UN had no problem condemning Israel for her completely justified response.[10] Words like *genocide* began to be used to describe not the actions of an **Islamic jihadi terrorist group**, but a recognized **sovereign state**, defending herself against an organization that describes itself as existing to destroy Israel.[11]

What about the Church?

In 2020, when the death of George Floyd in Minneapolis became the tipping point in America and made race the central conversation, pastors across our nation (me included) changed their plans, sermon series, and programming, and began to talk about what was taking place in that cultural moment.[12] This did not occur after October 7. In many churches and denominations, the silence was disconcerting. Regularly scheduled programming continued. For many, it was as if nothing had happened or was disconnected from their reality or what they saw as important. Very few voices stood up to address what had taken place in Israel and why it was important to those who profess to follow Jesus Christ. Even for those who gave it some attention, after a couple of weeks—with the war in Gaza only beginning and the protests erupting across Europe and the US—most just moved on. The interest had waned, and the attitude seemed to be best expressed in this common statement: "This happens over there *all* the time."

How could it be that the Church, which owes much to the Jewish people and the nation of Israel, possibly view such a horrendous culmination of hatred as unimportant or irrelevant? How could our hearts not be broken to the point of crying out in sackcloth and ashes? Was it indifference? Ignorance? Or something even more insidious?

I believe the answer for most of the Church is a combination of ignorance and indifference, as well as the presence of doctrinal error that has made our hearts cold toward the Jewish people and God's purposes and plans for the nation of Israel. A theology called **supersessionism,** or more commonly called *replacement theology* or *fulfillment theology,* has infected the Body of Christ. It's a belief that goes back to the early centuries of Christianity, which says that the Church, primarily made up of gentile believers, has now replaced Israel after the flesh and covenant promises God made to the descendants of Jacob. The gifts, promises, and calling of Israel, therefore, have been transferred to the Church.

Author and scholar in New Testament studies Gary Burge provides an example of what happens to God's Land promise to Israel when applying what could be seen as a supersessionism hermeneutic to Romans 4:13. Romans 4:13 reads, "For the promise to Abraham and his offspring that he would be heir of the world did not come through the law but through the righteousness of faith." Burge asserts:

The formula that linked Abraham to Jewish ethnic lineage and the right to possess the land has now been overturned in Christ. Paul's Christian theology links Abraham to children of faith, and to them belongs God's full domain, namely, the world.[13]

Author and professor of theology Michael J. Vlach does not "believe this understanding is biblical," for as he states, "Paul's main point in Romans 4:13 is about people who are descendants of Abraham, not land ... and ... universal blessings do not rule out particular blessings."[14]

Bestselling author and Bible teacher Joel Richardson rightly explains the problem with applying a supersessionist hermeneutic,

The supersessionist method of interpretation ... begins with the New Testament and then seeks to reinterpret or completely revise the original meaning of the Old Testament. Because supersessionists begin with the view that God is done with the Jews, when they look to the many promises made to the Jewish people throughout the Old Testament, they see a clear conflict with the New Testament. To resolve this, they turned to the Greek method of allegorizing or spiritualizing any passage in conflict with their supersessionist worldview.[15]

Vlach in his book *Has the Church Replaced Israel?* addresses the problem with these words:

If God is true and does not lie, how do we explain that He clearly promised certain things to a certain people but then fulfills them in a different manner than what He communicated? To say that God's ultimate fulfillment in the NT era is greater than what was promised in the OT does not escape this problem.[16]

J. C. Ryle, a nineteenth-century bishop, also wrote on the subject of "re-interpreting" the Old Testament in light of the New Testament. He took issue with "the habit of allegorizing plain sayings of the Word of God concerning the future history of the nation of Israel, and explaining away the fullness of the contents in order to accommodate them to the Gentile Church," claiming it was "unwarranted by Scripture."[17]

Sadly, supersessionism seems to fit well into the framework of how we Americans see our country and lives as the center of the universe. Conversely, we tend to see what takes place in the Middle East as not being all that important or even relevant. However, it only takes a brief survey of Church history to see how this erroneous doctrine has negatively affected the Church and created an almost impenetrable wall between Christians and Jews. Much of the antisemitism of the Middle Ages that led to massive persecution of Jews by the Church was inspired by this theology. Hitler himself utilized **Martin Luther**'s teaching, for example, to justify his (Hitler's) demonic pogroms and Holocaust.[18] Even in the best cases where replacement theology is passively embraced within denominational churches, the outcome has produced an attitude of *what's the big deal about Israel?*

This begs the question, why does Israel matter today? Why should we pay attention to this little nation the size of New Jersey with a population close to that of the state of Michigan —about 10 million people?

Make no mistake about it, Israel is not a side issue or cursory topic that we should leave to others to hash out. The Bible is an Israel-centric book. Jesus, Yeshua, is a glorified, Jewish man (fully God, fully man), and He is returning to rule the nations from Jerusalem.[19] *All redemptive history has its origin in the Land of Israel.* All the biblical, prophetic promises yet to be fulfilled will draw the attention of the world and cosmos back to this geography and this peculiar people.

You see, Israel is not going away. And as the end of the age approaches, she is going to become more and more relevant to the "todays" of our tomorrows as Satan rages against her and the Church, and the prophetic events of the Bible continue to unfold. We're only seeing the beginning of these things play out today in the news and on our media screens.

The Fallout Will Continue

In 2023, there was "an increase of 230% in antisemitic events worldwide compared to 2022."[20] The Hebrew University's Kantor Center for the Study of Contemporary European Jewry conducted research and found "an antisemitic incident occurs somewhere in the world every 80 seconds."[21] Then, of course, there's social media with its varied expressions of individual thought or opinion. An Israeli-based non-governmental organization (NGO) called Fighting Online Antisemitism, along with the **World Zionist Organization**, released a report that asserted, "Since the outbreak of the war, there has been a 300% spike in antisemitic content on social networks."[22]

It doesn't matter the day or date that you're reading this book. The fallout from October 7 is continuing and will continue. Why? How do I know this to be true? *Because October*

7 was a historical inflection point that has prophetic significance. On this day, Jewish hatred went mainstream. When antisemitism can be on full display online and in business, church, education, government, and the public square—and go pretty much unmitigated—it's become popular, common, the norm.

As I'm writing this, it's the summer of 2024. The '24 Summer Olympic Games have begun. And anti-Jewish-spewing, violent pro-Palestinian protests in Paris fill the streets as well as the news feeds. France reportedly took measures to ramp up security to "extreme levels ahead of [the] opening ceremony on the Seine River."[23] But even before the official ceremony kicked off, a preliminary soccer game between Israel and Mali showed signs of potential trouble. The crowd attending the game jeered as the Israeli national anthem was played, it also booed every time the Israeli team scored a goal against Mali's team, and some of the fans got into an argument that resulted in security having to intervene.[24]

During the same week, across the pond in the US, the replica of our nation's Liberty Bell "outside Washington, DC's Union Station was defaced with pro-Hamas symbols and anti-Israel messages ... during a protest against Netanyahu's speech," which I mentioned earlier in this chapter.[25] As if that were not enough, anti-Israel rioters burned the US flag and attempted to breach the US Capitol line that the US Capitol Police had formed to keep the rioters in place.[26] I actually saw the anti-Israel graffiti and signs from a car window as I drove by on my way to hear Prime Minister Netanyahu's landmark speech. I was a guest of Michigan Congressman Bill Huizenga, having received the invitation from him to attend the joint session of Congress. I'll never forget the sights I saw outside Union Station that day, neither will I forget being inside the

House Chamber and hearing Netanyahu unequivocally say, "For Israel, 'never again' must never be an empty promise. It must always remain a sacred vow. And after October 7th, 'never again' is now." Yet a few days after I heard these words, an Iranian-made Falaq-1 rocket hit a soccer field in Majdal Shams, the predominantly **Druze** town in the **Golan Heights**, killing 12 children and injuring more than 30 people. The IDF and US intelligence said Iran-backed **Hezbollah** was behind the attack even though Hezbollah denied responsibility.[27]

I could continue to chronicle public statements and events happening around the world as I write this, but perhaps the best way to underscore the antisemitic fallout that continues even as you read this book is to challenge you to look at your news feeds, watch the reports from various media outlets, and now let me ask you this: *Does Israel matter today—in your today?*

3

WHY ISRAEL MATTERS HISTORICALLY

Myth, legend, lore—these are the words that postmodern archaeologists and even biblical scholars have used to describe some of Israel's history as recounted in the Scripture. Why is that? Because they don't see the Bible as a reliable historical document. Walter C. Kaiser, Jr., in *A History of Israel,* explains,

> It has become increasingly common for scholars to see a difference between biblical Israel and historical Israel. Not long ago scholars generally believed that the Bible is a reasonably accurate depiction of Israel's history. Today, however, biblical Israel is viewed in many circles as a literary construction with little or no relationship to Israelite history.[1]

A postmodern approach like this, then, would not consider the Bible a primary source, if a source at all, of Israel's history. This means there are those in the fields of archaeology and biblical studies who view the patriarchs, the exodus from Egypt, and even the United Monarchy under King David as mere stories spun by a people to explain their origins. Thankfully, there are archaeologists and scholars who approach their research of Israel's history in a different way.

There are scholars who use the chronology and history of Israel "as set forth in the biblical text" as their "starting point and working assumption."[2] Such individuals have come to recognize there is much in archaeological research to support the **historicity** of the Bible and its recounting of Israel's history. What's more, "when the Bible is allowed to speak for itself and the archaeological data are properly understood, the archaeological evidence and the Bible record are in complete agreement."[3] I must interject here that, even among those using a postmodernist approach in their research, they have encountered archaeological evidence of some of the very things they have questioned in the biblical narrative.

What does all this have to do with addressing why Israel matters historically? When we examine the Jews' beginnings and their history as seen and explained in Scripture, and when we look at their prophetic promises and future also in Scripture, we can see their historical and theological relevance for all time. Moreover, *when we have archaeological support affirming the biblical history, which in turn lends credence to the biblical future, Israel's significance shines.*

It's important to note that there has been a tug of war between Israelis and Palestinians as to who was on the Land first and who has rightful ownership of territories like Gaza, the **West Bank**, and even Israel herself. It's critical, then, to have a basic understanding of the following:

- When did the Jewish people first live in the Land?
- Are there archaeological discoveries that appear to confirm the biblical narrative of Israel's history?
- What about other people groups, like the Palestinians, who have lived in the Land?

The Original Jewish Presence in the Land

Trying to find the first Jewish footprint today in the Land known as Israel has proven quite elusive to archaeologists and scholars. The evidence, as some describe it, "is almost always fragmentary and incomplete, especially the farther back in time one looks."[4] This is due to the complications related to the climate of the area, the many layers of debris from numerous civilizations that are present, and the buildings and structures currently standing atop potential archaeological sites. But we can look at the biblical record, using it as our starting point, and then look at the archaeological findings to get an idea of when the Jewish people first lived in the Land.

As we look to Genesis 12:5–6, we find the first mention of the patriarch Abraham (Abram) in the land of Canaan:

> Abram took Sarai his wife, and Lot his brother's son, and all their possessions that they had gathered, and the people that they had acquired in Haran, and they set out to go to the land of Canaan. When they came to the land of Canaan, Abram passed through the land to the place at Shechem, to the oak of Moreh. At that time the Canaanites were in the land.

Apparently, there was another group present in the Land when Abraham arrived. It was the Canaanites. But who were they? According to the **Table of Nations** in Genesis 10:6, 15, and 19, Canaan (the son of Ham) spread "his settlement to the Lebanese coastlands," and "in the **Tell el-Amarna tablets** of the 1300s BC, the people of this region are referred to as the *Kenaani* (Canaanites)."[5]

Although the Canaanites were there to "greet" Abraham, so to speak, the land of Canaan was promised to Abraham and his descendants along a certain family line. We'll get to that more specifically in a few pages. But here, in the Land we call Israel today, we read in Genesis 12 that the father of Judaism entered the land of Canaan for the first time.

Thankfully, there are a number of archaeological sites with finds that affirm "the antiquity of the narratives of Genesis" and contradict "claims that the story of Abraham was the fabrication of a group of priests living in Babylonian exile (or later) who created him to invent a glorious history for their people."[6] These sites and/or finds include:

- An oval from the relief from the temple wall of the Egyptian Pharaoh Shishak/Shoshenq I in the Negev that reads, "the Fort/Enclosure of Abram."[7]
- The Mari Tablets that contain names like Noah, Abram, Laban, and Jacob.[8]
- The Tomb of the Patriarchs in Hebron (the Cave of Machpelah) known to the Muslims as the Sanctuary of Abraham, that is considered a holy site in Christianity, Judaism, and Islam.[9]

When it comes to dating the year Abraham entered the Land, we run into disagreement, once again, among scholars. Some date the exodus from Egypt in the fifteenth century BC, while others date it in the thirteenth century BC. Of course, that affects dating the time of the patriarchs. For us lay people, the difference of a couple hundred years may not seem consequential, but to the shovel and trowel scientists, it matters!

All of this is beyond the scope of our abbreviated text here, but we can say that Abraham's arrival was somewhere around 2100 to 2000 BC. Purportedly, Abraham was born in 2166 BC, and when he was 75 years old, God called him to go to Canaan. That call would have been sometime in 2091 BC. Scripture tells us that Isaac was born in Canaan 25 years later (2066 BC) when Abraham was 100.[10] So a more accurate dating of Abraham's arrival in Canaan is between 2091 and 2066 BC.[11]

Now, I don't want to continue to do math calisthenics, and I'm sure you would appreciate my not making you do the same. Consequently, I've provided a chronology of Old Testament periods below along with dates for those periods.[12]

Biblical Periods Related to Israel

Period	Dates
Patriarchal	2166–1876 BC
Sojourn in Egypt	1876–1446 BC
Exodus & Wilderness	1446–1406 BC
Conquest of Canaan	1406–1371 BC
The Judges	1371–1049 BC
United Monarchy	1049–931 BC
The Divided Monarchy of Israel & Judah	931–587 BC
The Babylonian Exile & the Persian	587–334 BC
Intertestamental	400 BC–AD 25

What all this information tells us is the progenitor of the Jewish people stepped foot on the Land of Israel approximately 4,000 years ago. A Jewish presence in the Land has been there, barring some occasional trips to Egypt and the like due to famine and even bondage or slavery, a *very* long time.

God's Unilateral, Unconditional, Everlasting Covenant with Israel

To the most casual reader, it's obvious that the Old Testament is a telescopic story that begins with God choosing Abraham and then expanding His unilateral covenant promises to Abraham's descendants along the line of Isaac and Jacob (later renamed Israel). Israel, God's chosen people by sovereign election, is the subject of God's dealings in the Old Testament. *God's ultimate desire is that, through this covenant relationship, all the nations of the world would be blessed.*

> Now the Lord said to Abram, "Go from your country and your kindred and your father's house to the land that I will show you. And I will make of you a great nation, and I will bless you and make your name great, so that you will be a blessing. I will bless those who bless you, and him who dishonors you I will curse, and in you all the families of the earth shall be blessed."
>
> — GENESIS 12:1–3

> When the sun had gone down and it was dark, behold, a smoking fire pot and a flaming torch passed between these pieces. On that day the Lord made a covenant with Abram,

saying, "To your offspring I give this land, from the river of Egypt to the great river, the river Euphrates."

— GENESIS 15:17–18

God dealt with Israel unlike He did any other nation. Not because He was unfair or simply because she was His favorite, but because Israel had a special relationship (a covenant) and, therefore, a special responsibility. As the Israelites walked before the Lord according to His will and covenant, they experienced blessing. When they rebelled and went astray, God sent prophets and judged them. When they hardened their hearts and refused to hear His call to repentance, He would allow them to go into exile until such time as they once again called upon Him.

This judgment of exile was actually merciful, in that God would not allow them to change the conversation. Too much was at stake. Not just for Israel but for the world that would be the recipient of the overflow blessing through Israel as a light unto the nations. As God said to the Israelites through Moses, the great deliverer who led them to the Promised Land:

I call heaven and earth to witness against you today, that you will soon utterly perish from the land that you are going over the Jordan to possess. You will not live long in it, but will be utterly destroyed. And the Lord will scatter you among the peoples, and you will be left few in number among the nations where the Lord will drive you. And there you will serve gods of wood and stone, the work of human hands, that neither see, nor hear, nor eat, nor smell. But from there you will seek the Lord your God and you will find him, if you search after him with all your heart and with all your soul. When you are in tribulation, and all these things come upon you in the latter days, you will return to the Lord your God and obey his voice. For the Lord your God is a merciful God. He will not leave you or destroy you or forget the covenant with your fathers that he swore to them.

— DEUTERONOMY 4:26–31

Part of the covenant that God made with Abraham and with the descendant Jews was connected to the physical land of Canaan. God's goal for Israel was to be a servant nation to the other nations of the world. For them to be this kingdom of priests and a holy nation that would provoke the Gentiles unto jealousy and draw them, Israel had to be faithful. Her people could not become swept up into idolatry. Unfortunately, they were over and over again—even after the Twelve Tribes possessed the Land of their inheritance in Canaan.

When they were unfaithful, as the biblical text shows us, God removed them from the Land. When they repented, God restored them to the Land. *It was never an issue, though, or even a thought in God's mind that Israel would be permanently removed from the Land.* That was not His plan. We see God's intention in His covenantal encounter with Abraham.

When Abram was ninety-nine years old the Lord appeared to Abram and said to him, "I am God Almighty; walk before me, and be blameless, that I may make my covenant between me and you, and may multiply you greatly." Then Abram fell on his face. And God said to him, "Behold, my covenant is with you, and you shall be the father of a multitude of nations. No longer shall your name be called Abram, but your name shall be Abraham, for I have made you the father of a multitude of nations. I will make you exceedingly fruitful, and I will make you into nations, and kings shall come from you. And I will establish my covenant between me and you and your offspring after you throughout their generations for an everlasting covenant, to be God to you and to your offspring after you. And I will give to you and to your offspring after you the land of your sojournings, all the land of Canaan, for an everlasting possession, and I will be their God."

— GENESIS 17:1–8

The covenant at Sinai, the **Mosaic covenant**, was conditional, but the Abrahamic covenant was a unilateral covenant, one that God Himself had determined would be fulfilled. *Therefore, the deed to the Land would always belong to Israel and the Jewish people, because ultimately, God would Himself reign over the nations of the earth from this location, through the descendants of Abraham and Isaac.*

Later as the telescope of revelation comes more into focus through the Old Testament, we discover that the Messiah King would come through the line of David. God would re-establish His covenant with King David and further clarify His intentions to establish David's throne and kingdom forever. God promised David through the prophet Nathan:

I will raise up your offspring after you, who shall come from your body, and I will establish his kingdom. He shall build a house for my name, and I will establish the throne of his kingdom forever. I will be to him a father, and he shall be to me a son. When he commits iniquity, I will discipline him with the rod of men, with the stripes of the sons of men, but my steadfast love will not depart from him, as I took it from Saul, whom I put away from before you. And your house and your kingdom shall be made sure forever before me. Your throne shall be established forever.

— 2 SAMUEL 7:12–16

This not only is central to the prophetic scriptures throughout the rest of the Old Testament, but it is realized in the coming of the Messiah, Jesus Christ, who is both the son of David by physical lineage and the Son of God by miraculous incarnation. The apostle Paul spoke of this when he opened his letter to the Romans:

Paul, a servant of Christ Jesus, called to be an apostle, set apart for the gospel of God, which he promised beforehand through his prophets in the holy Scriptures, concerning his Son, who was descended from David according to the flesh and was declared to be the Son of God in power according to the Spirit of holiness by his resurrection from the dead, Jesus Christ our Lord.

— ROMANS 1:1–4

The Gospels describe how Jesus came to His people and, in large part, was rejected. His signs, teaching, and ultimately His resurrection from the dead validated His claim to be the Son of God and the rightful King even though only a remnant of Israel received Him. *Jesus would build His new community with twelve foundation stones of Jewish apostles, sending them out into the nations with the gospel proclamation of the Kingdom of God.*

> He came to his own, and his own people did not receive him. But to all who did receive him, who believed in his name, he gave the right to become children of God.
>
> — JOHN 1:11–12

The fourfold promise in the Abrahamic covenant of (1) offspring, (2) Land, (3) God's blessing upon Abraham, and (4) the blessing of the nations through him is in perpetuity. You and I have been blessed by the seed of Abraham and the history of his descendants. We have become children of God because of that Seed.

Three Important Archaeological Finds

Though we dated Abraham's arrival in Canaan somewhere between 2100 and 2000 BC, most scholars can agree that Jewish people have lived in the Land that is today made up of Israel and Palestinian-controlled territory for over 3,500 years. Even during the **diaspora**, there has always been a remnant of Jews living in their ancestral homeland. This is not just an assertion made by Jewish and Christian leaders. Archaeologists continue to discover evidence of Israel's presence in the Land as well as evidence corroborating the biblical history of Israel.

An early stele, known as the Merneptah Stele, was discovered in Thebes, Egypt, in 1896. A stele is a stone or wooden slab that serves as a monument of the ancient world. Typically, it is decorated with text, hieroglyphs, figures, or some other ornamentation. The Merneptah Stele "is sometimes referred to as the 'Israel Stele' because a majority of scholars translate a set of hieroglyphs in line 27 as 'Israel.'"[13] This seems to support the notion that there was an Israel as far back as around 1208 BC when this stele was created.

Possibly the most well-known archaeological find are the **Dead Sea Scrolls** in Qumran. "For thousands of years the Judaean Desert held secrets buried in its sands, only to be revealed by a young Bedouin shepherd in 1947."[14] The scrolls contained parts of the Hebrew Bible, with every book being represented except the book of Esther, and verified the wording and meaning of the modern rendering of the Old Testament.

Sometime during the eighteenth century BC, a huge city gate was constructed on the eastern side of Dan, which is located in northern Israel. Excavations began there at what is called Tel Dan in 1963, and the gate, as I mentioned previously, was known as "Abraham's Gate." In 1993, a slab or stele fragment was discovered at the site with an Aramaic inscription that translated, "house of David."[15] This is considered the first historical evidence of the biblical David.

These are only three of the very many pieces of evidence that support the Bible's narrative, and even more findings come to light annually. These also underscore the validity of Israel's history as a people and geopolitical nation. As archaeologist Dr. Scott Stripling has said, "After 150 years of archaeology in Israel, hundreds of synchronisms (connections) between the material culture and the biblical text have been established. At this point, it takes more faith to believe that the Bible is not true than to believe that it is true."[16]

What about the Palestinians?

Despite this bedrock evidence, Palestinian organizations and Arab leaders are fond of arguing that there is very little to no indicators Jews ever lived en masse within the borders of modern-day Israel. A real propaganda machine is behind this, constantly attempting to undermine Israel's rightful and historical claim to the Land. Regardless of the attempts made to wipe away a few thousand years of history, the fact remains that up until AD 70, when the Roman Emperor **Titus** destroyed the Temple in Jerusalem, razed the city, and killed thousands of Jews, taking thousands more back into the nations as slaves,* Israel was a historically known and occupied nation. This historical ethnic cleansing and scattering of the Jewish people is portrayed on the **Arch of Titus**, standing today on the Via Sacra in Rome.

But the question remains, should the Jewish people have a right to live in their ancestral homeland, especially after such a long period of time has elapsed, and the Palestinians not be allowed theirs—not be allowed self-determination and self-governance?

First, it's important to recognize that, even though the Jewish people were killed, exiled, and transported into Europe as slaves, we must not forget that a remnant did remain. Titus's

---

* Scholars differ on the exact number of deaths and captives. Josephus asserted as many as 1.1 million people were killed with 97,000 Jews being taken into captivity.

actions in AD 70 were in response to a Judaean rebellion against Rome. In fact, that revolt from AD 66–70, or the First Jewish-Roman War, was one of the most serious. Other Jewish leaders and revolutionaries rebelled against the Romans in the years that followed the destruction of Jerusalem. There was the **Kitos War** of AD 115–117 and the **Bar Kokhba Revolt** in AD 132–136, for example. These were carried out by Jewish patriots who had survived, remained in the Land, and continued to push against the Romans, but both of these revolts were crushed by the Romans. Yet, there has never been a time that a significant population of Jewish people did not live on or in proximity to the Land that was given to them as an everlasting inheritance from the God of their forefathers.

Second, it's also important to realize that, historically, there is no specific group of people with a distinct ethnicity known as Palestinians. Most of those who today are called Palestinians have either Arab backgrounds or are a mixture of Syrian, Jordanian (biblically known as Edomites and Moabites, respectively), and the people around the Land of Israel during the period of time in which the colonial expansion of Islam was taking place. My friend Avner Boskey does a great job tracing and explaining this in his book *Jews, Arabs, & the Middle East: A Messianic Perspective.* He states that the General Assembly of the UN declared the existence of the Palestinian people:

On December 10, 1969, the General Assembly ratified Resolution 2535 (XXIV) United Nations Relief ad Works Agency for Palestine Refugees in the Near East. There it defined the existence of a "Palestinian" people, asserted that this people had "inalienable rights" and declared that Israel was denying Palestinians these rights through illegally occupying "their" territories.

In one fell swoop on the banks of New York City's East River a Palestinian people was created. The UN had decided! Who cares what happened in Jewish and biblical history? Who cares about the Greek national origins of the Philistines? Who cares about the ethnic cleansing of the Jews of Israel which was carried out by Islam's jihad armies? Never mind that there has never ever been a country called **"Palestine"** or a citizenship with that name. Never mind that barely thirty years before, the term "Palestinian" could mean "Jew" just as easily as it could mean "Arab." The assembled nations of the world lit a fuse that day without understanding the bomb was strapped to their own chests.[17]

Third, the people who are called Palestinians today are caught in the crossfire of this conflict. We have brothers and sisters, Palestinian Christians, who live in Gaza and the West Bank. There are many Palestinian Muslims in these territories who want to live their lives peacefully, and if given an option, they would work to do so. In fact, they have worked to do so. There are Arabs and Palestinians who live peacefully within Israel, coming and going to work, to the markets, and to the mosque or synagogue of their choice to worship. Arabs even serve in the **Knesset** government of Israel. As we will see in the next chapter, Israel has endeavored to negotiate paths for a peaceful coexistence, wanting to allow for Palestinians to continue to live in the PTOs. The real problem is the infiltration of terrorist organizations like Hamas or other Iranian-backed groups using Palestinians as military camouflage as well as human shields.

Yet it's Israel that possesses a covenantal promise from God that affirms her claim to the Land. There is archaeological evidence of the biblical historical record of the people and nation. Together, this affirms *Israel matters historically.*

4

WHY ISRAEL MATTERS POLITICALLY

Israel has a national history—a geopolitical history—in the Land, giving her political legitimacy. Although this is not necessarily an issue that has religious or theological roots, having a clear understanding of the political realities does play into our ability to see the full picture.

Since the October 7th attack against Israel and the continued onslaught by Hamas, Hezbollah, **Houthis**, and other proxy groups for the **Islamic Republic of Iran**, the reaction of the global community toward Israel's response, as we discussed in chapter 2, has been nothing short of shocking. There has been very little international sympathy expressed. In fact, the opposite has occurred. In May of 2024, Prime Minister Benjamin Netanyahu as well as his Defense Minister **Yoav Gallant** were accused of "war crimes and crimes against humanity since October 2023" by the **International Criminal Court (ICC)**.[1] The ICC actually requested arrest warrants be issued. Can you imagine this being done to leaders of any other nation in the free world?

The insidious head of antisemitism has arrogantly risen in a way that we have not seen since World War 2 and the days of the Holocaust. That same insidious spirit has seeped into the political arena in which the validity or legitimacy of Israel as a sovereign nation is now openly called into question, or in an even stronger way, denounced with the mantra *"From the river to the sea, Palestine shall be free."* This statement is not simply something chanted by aspirational protestors who are looking for peaceful coexistence. It has long served as

> a rallying cry for terrorist groups and their sympathizers, from the **Popular Front for the Liberation of Palestine** to Hamas, which called for Israel's destruction in its original governing charter in 1988.... [The mantra] calls for the establishment of a State of Palestine from the Jordan River to the Mediterranean Sea, erasing the State of Israel and its people. Another phrase "Globalize the **Intifada**," which uses the Arabic word for "uprising" or "shaking off," also calls for widespread violence against both Israelis and Jews across the globe.[2]

In essence, this call for Palestine to take control of the entire territory of Israel is propagating the idea that Israel doesn't have a rightful, political claim. Moreover, those who use the mantra see Jews as colonizers of their "Palestinian land" who must be removed—even exterminated. This begs the questions:

- Do any of the other nations have a legitimate geopolitical claim to the Land?

- Does Israel have an existential right to exist and defend her current borders?

The Diaspora: Jews Dispersed into the Nations

After the events of AD 70, Jews were dispersed into the nations, migrating "across North Africa, through Asia Minor, and on into Europe. Wherever they went, they formed small communities."[3] Some Jews even ended up in America as "the first Jewish residents of New Amsterdam, on what we call Manhattan."[4] And though they were able to establish and even flourish in those communities, "they were increasingly subjected to discrimination, forced conversion, physical violence, and finally, exile."[5]

Throughout the centuries, Jewish exiles experienced all the history associated with the various lands to which they had migrated. No matter where they went or what they lived through, somehow they became the scapegoat for what was going on around them. On the continent of Europe, there were the Saxon Wars (772–804), the Viking invasions (793–1066), the Norman Conquest (1066–1071), the Hundred Years' War (1337–1453), the Spanish Inquisition (1478–1834), and even the Black Death of the late Middle Ages. Meanwhile, back in the Land of Israel, Jews still there lived through various ruling empires like the Roman (lasted into the 300s), Byzantine (313–636), Arab (636–1099), Crusader (1099–1260), Mamluk (1260–1517), Ottoman (1517–1917), and British (1917–1948).

Notice there was no Palestinian rule of the Holy Land. As far as what is known today as Palestine, it was a term "used for millennia without a precise geographic definition.... Since the

Roman era, the name lacked political significance. No nation ever had that name."[6] What's more,

> "Palestine" applied vaguely to a region that for the 400 years before World War I was part of the Ottoman Empire. In that empire, it was divided among several provinces and governates and never composed an administrative unit.[7]

Historically, there has never been a sovereign Palestine. And Israel has never been under a "Palestinian" rule. As far as some indigenous people group having claim to the Land of Israel is concerned, the real evidence supports the Jewish people's claim as being indigenous to the Land.

Nineteenth-Century Zionism

More and more, European Jews were experiencing antisemitic treatment in the nineteenth century. With nationalism rising in European countries to establish nation-states based on shared values, culture, history, and language, Jews were finding themselves being ostracized and enduring greater restrictions.

While the circumstances of the Jewish people were deteriorating in Europe, hope for a return to their homeland was growing as **Theodor Herzl** and other like-minded Jewish thinkers saw the hour as an opportunity to call for the creation of a Jewish state. In 1896, Herzl wrote a pamphlet entitled *A Jewish State: An Attempt at a Modern Solution of the Jewish Question* to issue that call. He said, "The idea which I have developed in this pamphlet is a very old one: the restoration of the

Jewish State. The earth resounds with outcries against the Jews, and the outcries have awakened the slumbering idea."[8] With his vision of an independent Jewish state, the Zionist movement was born.

The argument is often made that the Jewish population in the Ottoman-controlled territory of Palestine was minuscule, and that it wasn't until the rise of **Zionism** in Europe during the nineteenth century that European Jews began to make **aliyah** and migrate to their ancestral homeland. According to this argument, the vast majority of the population in the 1800s was made of Arabs, and with the infusion of Jews, the Arabs' land, homes, and jobs began to be taken over. This argument is revisionist at best and does not accurately portray the reality of the situation leading up to the decisive twentieth century. Alan Dershowitz, the Felix Frankfurter Professor of Law at Harvard Law School, explains, "The Jews of the First Aliyah did not displace local residents by conquest or fear as the Americans and Australians did. They lawfully and openly bought land from the 1880s to the present."[9] Besides, as he contends, "International treaties and law recognized that the Jewish community in Palestine was there, as a matter 'of right.'"[10]

Though the number of Jewish immigrants moving back to the Land of Israel increased exponentially during the nineteenth century, the same can be said about their Arab neighbors who did not until recently identify themselves as Palestinian. By the year 1914, the estimated Jewish population in the Land was roughly 94,000 out of a total population of 689,000. By 1948, the number of Jews would grow to over 700,000 as a result of the Jewish emigration from Europe as well as surrounding Arab neighboring nations, where Jews had lived for hundreds and even a few thousand years.[11]

With the increase of tension between the burgeoning State of Israel and its Arab neighbors, those Jewish residents were either encouraged or, for their own safety, decided it best to move out of places like Transjordan, Yemen, Iraq, and Syria as a result of persecution. The aspirations of self-determination as a people gained momentum not only in Europe and America, but throughout the Middle East, causing many Jewish people to long for an ultimate home-land in the place where their ancestors once dwelt. As more Jews returned to the Land of Promise, they created several Jewish settlements throughout the Land as well as devel-oped cities and farms, and what were once malaria-ridden swamps started to be transformed into orange groves. The first city was Tel Aviv.

As the settlements began to swell and take on a civil iden-tity of their own, Arabs also began to move to Israel for the jobs that were now being made available. It is important to understand that, up until this time, the territory known as Palestine was under Turkish (Ottoman) control. It would be the First World War that changed the geopolitical landscape and shifted authority over to the British Empire.

The Balfour Declaration

The Balfour Declaration of 1917 set the stage for a legally recognized Jewish state to exist. After the defeat of the Ottoman Empire, control of the territory and the determina-tion of how to manage it was handed over to the British. As Dershowitz states:

World War I pitted the British (among others) against the Germans and the Ottoman Empire (among others). The United States entered the war on the British side in 1917, and President Woodrow Wilson declared that the principle of self-determination should govern any postwar reorganization of territories that were formerly controlled by the Ottoman Empire. Support for Jewish self-determination in those areas of Palestine in which Jews constituted a majority was seen by many as part of Wilsonian self-determination. [12]

The British saw this as an opportunity to recognize not just a single state (giving all of it to either the Arabs or the Jews, or even to Syria), but a serendipitous moment to establish both a Jewish homeland and a Arab Palestinian state not ruled by Syria or any other nation. 80 percent of the Palestinian territory would be given exclusively to the formation of an Arab state in which there would be no Jewish settlements. That nation became known as Transjordan (today called Jordan).

At that time, it was internationally recognized that the Jewish population was "in Palestine by right," and that it was the responsibility of the international community to not only recognize but foster the formation of a Jewish national home —and not just for those Jews who were already living in the Land, but even for those who were currently living elsewhere. It was agreed that they should be strongly encouraged to come and join in this formation of a Jewish state.

Many developments and attempts to see both an Arab state and a Jewish state peacefully coexist in Palestine were made over the next few decades. It would take a Holocaust of over 6 million Jews in Germany to bring the issue to a head for the international community.

A Jewish Nation Is Born *Again*

On May 14, 1948, **David Ben-Gurion**, who would become Israel's first prime minister, announced the establishment of the State of Israel. The population of Jews living in the Land had swollen from 100,000 at the beginning of World War 1 now to more than 800,000. Many Jews from Europe and America had responded to the invitation to make aliyah to the Land of Promise. Israel could finally answer the question—"Can these bones live?"—with a resounding, "Yes!"

The US was the first nation to recognize Israel as a legitimate nation. This triggered an immediate response from Israel's Arab neighbors. After months of war following the UN release of its partition plan of 1947—which called for the partition of Palestine into Arab and Jewish States with special oversight of Jerusalem by Jordan, Saudi Arabia, the US, and the state of Palestine—the **Arab League** declared war against the new Jewish State. Their determination to wipe Israel off the map was demonstrated by the assault the next morning by Egypt, Transjordan (Jordan), Syria, and Iraq. While it seemed that Israel was vastly outnumbered by their Arab enemies, this would be a war that they had to win, and they did.

The Original Two-State Solution

Those who today argue for a "two-state solution" are either uninformed or forgetting that there already is a two-state solution that has been established from the very beginning. Those who contend that there should be an additional Palestinian state are actually arguing for a "three-state solution." The difficulty in this whole process over the last 80 years is that, despite there already being 21 Arab States surrounding Israel, making up a geographical area about the size of the continental US, leaders representing the Palestinian people have refused offers made to them to form a separate, sovereign state alongside Israel. Their goal is not a two-state solution, but it would seem they are committed to a "No Jew Solution."

In 1937, the Arabs rejected the **Peel Commission**'s goal for a two-state solution.[13] In 1947, they once again rejected the UN partition plan that would have created two separate states. It's ironic that, when Israel declared herself a new nation, the Arabs declared war against Israel and actually lost more land as a result than they would have gained had they accepted the terms of the UN partition plan.

Many years later, after several wars with her Arab neighbors, Israel came to the bargaining table at the bequest of US President Bill Clinton at the 2000 **Camp David Summit. Ehud Barak**, then prime minister of Israel, offered **Yasser Arafat**, chairman of the **Palestine Liberation Organization (PLO)** and president of the **Palestinian Authority (PA)**, Palestinian statehood in Gaza and 94 percent of the West Bank, with East Jerusalem as its capital. A quite generous offer in exchange for peace, and yet, Arafat and the PA rejected this offer, instead initiating the **Second Intifada.**

In 2005, Israel pulled out of Gaza, turning over total control of this territory. With international support and aid, the PA had the opportunity to build the infrastructure for a future state. Instead, they elected Hamas, a terrorist organization committed to the destruction of Israel. In 2008, Israel offered **Mahmoud Abbas** everything that was offered at Camp David. Yet, again, the offer was rejected. It became apparent that Palestinians under Hamas were not interested in building a "second state" but would only be satiated if every Jew was murdered or removed and the State of Israel ceased to exist.

An Abbreviated Chronology

Event	Scripture
First Aliyah into *Eretz Israel* from Russia	1881
First Zionist Congress	1897
Outbreak of World War 1 Turkish Ottoman Outlaws Zionism	1914
The Balfour Declaration	1917
The British Mandate	1920
Hitler Instigates Program of Antisemitism across Germany	1934
Peel Commission	1936
World War 2 The Holocaust	1939–1945
UN Partition Plan	1947
Israel's War of Independence	1948
Sinai War	1956
Creation of the PLO	1964
Six-Day War	1967
Camp David Accords	1979
First Intifada	1987–1993
Oslo Accords	1993
Second Intifada	2000–2005
Israel's Withdrawal from the Gaza Strip	2005
Hamas De Facto Governing of Gaza	2007
Abraham Accords	2020
Israel-Hamas War	2023

1967—The Turning Point

I want to close out this chapter by revisiting what I believe was the real turning point for Israel since her recognized statehood in 1948. It was the **Six-Day War**. On June 5, 1967, Israel launched a preemptive strike against Egypt after persistent conflicts and threats by Egyptian President **Gamal Nasser**. Eventually, Jordan and Syria joined the fight against Israel. After just six days of battle, not only did Israel survive the assault from three sides, but the nation actually gained the **Sinai Peninsula**, Gaza, the Golan Heights, and the Jordanian annexed West Bank, including East Jerusalem. This was the first time Jerusalem was under Jewish control since its destruction in AD 70.

The political and prophetic significance of this moment cannot be overstated. The very words that Jesus had prophesied about Jerusalem becoming restored to Jewish hands in the last days took place just over fifty years ago:

> They will fall by the edge of the sword and be led captive into all the nations, and Jerusalem will be trampled under foot by the Gentiles, until the times of the Gentiles are fulfilled.
>
> — LUKE 21:24

Jesus indicated that the recapture of Jerusalem from gentile (non-Jewish) hands would mark a turning point in both the history of Israel and the world. No other nation has existed in the history of the world that has been destroyed and scattered, has returned into its homeland, and has been reborn. Israel stands alone as a political sign and a wonder. That's *why Israel matters politically.*

5

WHY ISRAEL MATTERS
THEOLOGICALLY

E ven more important than the historical and political records, which confirm the birth and ongoing existence of Israel, is the theological framework that buttresses her history as well as her future. Without seeing how God's purposes and covenant faithfulness are played out through His elect people, her historical record, albeit with archeological proof, and her political legitimacy will only relegate Israel to the ash heap of other civilizations like Babylon, Greece, Assyria, and Persia. The modern political turmoil and controversy can be ignored or, worse, considered a twenty-first-century coincidence if we do not grasp the sovereign hand of the Lord preserving and guiding the Jewish people from the scattered nations back into their ancestral Land by covenant at the end of the age.

In chapter 3, we reviewed the Abrahamic and Mosaic covenants. In this chapter, we want to consider what the Bible has to say regarding the promises of Israel's future, which are the theological premises of the last days. We will consider:

- Is God finished with Israel?
- What promises has God made in the Scripture concerning Israel that are yet to be fulfilled?
- How is the regathering of Jews to the Land of Israel related to end-time events?

God Is Not Finished with Israel

Even though by and large the Jewish people did not receive their Messiah due to their false expectations of how He would come and reestablish the Kingdom, God's purposes and promises to Abraham remain intact. *In fact, God will fulfill all His covenant promises to Israel proclaimed in Scripture.*

In AD 70, Israel was taken captive into the nations of the earth and her Temple destroyed. This exile was longer and more extensive than previous periods of judgment. The rejection of the Messiah came with greater ramifications, resulting in a partial hardening and spiritual blinding taking place.

> What then? Israel failed to obtain what it was seeking. The elect obtained it, but the rest were hardened, as it is written, "God gave them a spirit of stupor, eyes that would not see and ears that would not hear, down to this very day."
>
> — ROMANS 11:7–8

In the natural, it seemed as if God had forsaken His people and completely rejected them. This hardening occurred as the New Covenant was being spread to the Gentiles for over 2,000 years, fulfilling God's eternal purposes from the beginning through His faithful Son and descendant of Abraham, Isaac,

Jacob, *and* David. If that had been the end of the story, we could easily say today that Israel, after the flesh, no longer matters or plays a significant part in our current moment or future. But Scripture shows us that this is not the case:

> I ask, then, has God rejected his people? By no means! For I myself am an Israelite, a descendant of Abraham, a member of the tribe of Benjamin. God has not rejected his people whom he foreknew. Do you not know what the Scripture says of Elijah, how he appeals to God against Israel? "Lord, they have killed your prophets, they have demolished your altars, and I alone am left, and they seek my life." But what is God's reply to him? "I have kept for myself seven thousand men who have not bowed the knee to Baal." So too at the present time there is a remnant, chosen by grace.
>
> — ROMANS 11:1–5

The Promise of Return

In the mystery of God's eternal purposes and election, He has promised unconditionally to return His attention to the Jewish people and bring them back from the farthest corners of the nations. He will deal with them one final time until His controversy with Jacob is resolved.

Isaiah 34:8 (KJ21) declares, "For it is the day of the Lord's vengeance, and the year of recompenses for the controversy of Zion." This controversy of Zion is the ever present and consistent frustrations of the nations over the Jewish people themselves, the Land given by covenant, and more specifically, the city of Jerusalem. The controversy is God dealing with the nations while also dealing with His people until they are finally faithful to Him.

One of the most significant prophecies fulfilled from the Scriptures is the recent return of Jews from the nations back into the Land of Promise and the restoration of their national identity. Prophesied thousands of years ago, we have seen and will continue to see one of the greatest miracles witnessed in human history: *God bringing His people back into the Land of Israel from the farthest corners of the nations as the world is nearing the return of Messiah Jesus at the end of the age.* The recent return of Jews from the nations is even more miraculous when we realize that their return is while they are still in the state of unbelief. God has sovereignly gathered them for the purpose of His ultimate dealing with His covenant people.

When we read the prophets speaking about the future return of God's covenant people to the Land, there are some scriptures that seem to indicate a return after they acknowledge the Messiah and receive the spirit of grace and supplication, and other verses that seem to indicate they return in unbelief before they acknowledge their King. Consider this prophecy in Ezekiel 36:24–27:

> I will take you from the nations and gather you from all the countries and bring you into your own land. I will sprinkle clean water on you, and you shall be clean from all your uncleannesses, and from all your idols I will cleanse you. And I will give you a new heart, and a new spirit I will put within you. And I will remove the heart of stone from your flesh and give you a heart of flesh. And I will put my Spirit within you, and cause you to walk in my statutes and be careful to obey my rules.

Notice it isn't until they have come back into the Land that God cleanses them from their sin and puts His Spirit within them, both of which evidence the New Covenant. It is striking to realize that part of God's sovereign plan to save *all Israel* is to actually bring her back into the Land to once again capture her attention, even in her unbelief. The regathering of Israel at the end of the age will trigger the prophetic timeline, accelerating events toward the time Jeremiah referred to as "the time of Jacob's trouble," in the King James Version, or "a time of distress for Jacob" below in the ESV:

> These are the words that the Lord spoke concerning Israel and Judah: "Thus says the Lord: We have heard a cry of panic, of terror, and no peace. Ask now, and see, can a man bear a child? Why then do I see every man with his hands on his stomach like a woman in labor? Why has every face turned pale? Alas! That day is so great there is none like it; it is a time of distress for Jacob; yet he shall be saved out of it.
>
> — JEREMIAH 30:4–7

For many of the Old Testament prophecies to come to pass, the Jewish people must be present in the Land. This current regathering and that which will continue are in preparation. For Jesus to ultimately return to a Jewish Jerusalem, it is necessary that Jerusalem be under the control of the Jewish people. It will be in Jerusalem where God will pour on the city's inhabitants "a spirit of grace":

> And I will pour out on the house of David and the inhabitants of Jerusalem a spirit of grace and pleas for mercy, so

that, when they look on me, on him whom they have pierced, they shall mourn for him, as one mourns for an only child, and weep bitterly over him, as one weeps over a firstborn.

— ZECHARIAH 12:10

The return to Jerusalem, Israel's eternal capital, occurred in 1967 and will continue until the day that the whole house of David shall look upon Jesus the Messiah.

All Israel Will Be Saved and Re-Grafted In

In Romans 11, Paul addressed the issue of the natural branches (Israel after the flesh) being cut off because of their unbelief. For many Christians, this becomes the end of the story, but that was not where Paul left off because it was not where God's purposes for Israel terminate.

In Romans 11:12, Paul said, "Now if their transgression is riches for the world and their failure is riches for the Gentiles, how much more will their fulfillment be!" Paul was making it very clear that, as much as God had judged Israel for her unbelief by cutting her off, it was only temporary because there will come a time of restoration in which these natural branches are grafted back in. And this will be a more significant event than Israel's removal was. Paul literally called the failure and transgression of Israel, "riches."

In verse 18 of Romans 11, Paul warned the gentile believers, whom he described as the "wild olive branches"—ones who have been grafted in *unnaturally*—to not become arrogant toward the Jewish people. If God did not spare them for their unbelief, the same could happen to you and me. Interestingly, the sin that is most connected to looking down upon the Jewish people or dismissing the promises that God made to them covenantal through Abraham is described as arrogance. I see this in so many theological streams throughout the history of the Church. Unfortunately, in many cases, it has led to antisemitism, persecution of Jews, and hindered Christian-Jewish relationships that could have resulted in salvation among the Jewish people.

In verse 15, Paul described this time of restoration of the natural branches as *life back from the dead*. This is describing the mass conversion of the Jewish people at the end of the age as a sort of resurrection. We know that the resurrection from the dead is the single greatest miracle that confirmed the Lordship and Messiahship of Jesus Christ. It literally changed the perspective and lives of the original disciples, giving them the conviction and courage to lay down their lives for the sake of the gospel. It seems that the salvation of Israel during the last period of human history, referred to as the time of Jacob's trouble, will be a miracle like unto the resurrection. It brings to mind the following prophecy given in Ezekiel 37:3-6:

> And he said to me, "Son of man, can these bones live?" And I answered, "O Lord God, you know." Then he said to me, "Prophesy over these bones, and say to them, O dry bones, hear the word of the Lord. Thus says the Lord God to these bones: Behold, I will cause breath to enter you, and you shall live. And I will lay sinews upon you, and will cause flesh to come upon you, and cover you with skin, and put breath in you, and you shall live, and you shall know that I am the Lord."

Jesus Christ Will Reign from Jerusalem

Israel matters because Jerusalem matters. Jerusalem is intricately connected to the promise God made to David that He would establish David's throne forever and install one of David's descendants upon that throne. This is referred to as the Davidic covenant but, in reality, is a progressive revelation of the covenant that God originally made with Abraham. This throne will be set in the city limits of Jerusalem, the city of the great King—the city that Jesus wept over and prophesied that, when the inhabitants see Him again, they will receive Him fully. This covenant of David as well as Abraham was far more than an allegorical play on words by God. It had literal, physical implications, not just to a spiritual seed or spiritual benefits alone, but including the actual Land as an everlasting possession, beginning with Jerusalem. We read:

> I will raise up your offspring after you, who shall come from your body, and I will establish his kingdom. He shall build a house for my name, and I will establish the throne of his kingdom forever. I will be to him a father, and he shall be to me a son. When he commits iniquity, I will discipline him with the rod of men, with the stripes of the sons of men, but my steadfast love will not depart from him.
>
> — 2 SAMUEL 7:12–15

Jesus is the obvious fulfillment of this promise, confirmed by all of the writers of the New Testament.[1] In fact, the most quoted Psalm in all of the New Testament deals with the throne.

The Lord says to my Lord: "Sit at my right hand, until I make
your enemies your footstool." The Lord sends forth from
Zion your mighty scepter. Rule in the midst of your enemies!

— PSALM 110:1–2

The disciples asked Jesus about this during the forty-day
period of time after the resurrection in which He was teaching
them about the Kingdom of God and what was to come. They
obviously were expecting a physical restoration of the
kingdom of Israel with the Messiah (Jesus) reigning from
Jerusalem. As Scripture tells us:

So when they had come together, they asked him, "Lord, will
you at this time restore the kingdom to Israel?" He said to
them, "It is not for you to know times or seasons that the
Father has fixed by his own authority. But you will receive
power when the Holy Spirit has come upon you, and you will
be my witnesses in Jerusalem and in all Judea and Samaria,
and to the end of the earth."

— ACTS 1:6–8

Another Old Testament prophecy foreseeing the Messiah
sitting and ruling over the nations from the throne of David is
found in Isaiah 9. This oft quoted passage during Advent or
the Christmas season is unfortunately spiritualized and
stripped of its literal future fulfillment when Jesus Christ
returns to the earth to rule and reign for 1,000 years.

For to us a child is born, to us a son is given; and the government shall be upon his shoulder, and his name shall be called Wonderful Counselor, Mighty God, Everlasting Father, Prince of Peace. Of the increase of his government and of peace there will be no end, on the throne of David and over his kingdom, to establish it and to uphold it with justice and with righteousness from this time forth and forevermore. The zeal of the Lord of hosts will do this.

— ISAIAH 9:6–7

The number of prophetic scriptures pointing toward this future restoration of Israel as a special nation, serving the other nations under the leadership of Jesus, is too great to quote here. Allow me to quote two final prophecies that clearly indicate this:

Behold, the days are coming, declares the Lord, when I will fulfill the promise I made to the house of Israel and the house of Judah. In those days and at that time I will cause a righteous Branch to spring up for David, and he shall execute justice and righteousness in the land. In those days Judah will be saved, and Jerusalem will dwell securely. And this is the name by which it will be called: "The Lord is our righteousness."

— JEREMIAH 33:14–16

It shall come to pass in the latter days that the mountain of the house of the Lord shall be established as the highest of the mountains, and shall be lifted up above the hills; and all

the nations shall flow to it, and many peoples shall come, and
say: "Come, let us go up to the mountain of the Lord, to the
house of the God of Jacob, that he may teach us his ways and
that we may walk in his paths." For out of Zion shall go forth
the law, and the word of the Lord from Jerusalem. He shall
judge between the nations, and shall decide disputes for
many peoples; and they shall beat their swords into plow-
shares, and their spears into pruning hooks; nation shall not
lift up sword against nation, neither shall they learn war
anymore.

— ISAIAH 2:2–4

The present and future regathering of Israel is important
to the future prophetic purposes of God. It has nothing to do
with the deservedness of the Jewish people, just like salvation
for Gentiles and all people alike is due to God's grace and not
our works or merit. *The unconditional election of the Jewish
people is significant because it is God's wisdom put on full display
through the redemptive arc of Israel throughout the millennia, and
it is His covenant faithfulness in the face of consistent unfaithfulness
by Israel that ultimately breaks down the barriers of her unbelief
and woos her to Himself.*

Almost 4,000 years later, God has still bound Himself to
the promise He made to Abraham. God's regathering of Jews
from the four winds of the nations back to their homeland
should serve as a signpost of the prophetic hour in which we
are living, as the chart on the next page of important end-time
events further illustrates.

End-Time Events

Event	Scripture(s)
Beginnings of the regathering of Jews back to the Land	Isa 43:5–6; Jer 16:14–15; 23:3, 7–8; 29:14; 31:7–8; Ezek 11:17; 37:21
Rebirth of the State of Israel (1948)	Isa 66:8
Large scale return to the Land	Isa 11:11–12
Recapture of the city of Jerusalem (1967)	Joel 3:1; Zech 12:6
Beginning of the birth pangs—increased war, conflict, deception	Matt 24; Mark 13; Luke 21; 1 Tim 4:1
Increased persecution for the gospel's sake	Matt 24:9–10; Mark 13:11–13; Luke 21:12–19
Gospel advancing throughout the nations by the Church	Matt 24:14; Mark 13:10
Increased global crisis over the issue of Israel	Ps 83; Zech 12:2–3
Emergence of the antichrist	Dan 7:24–27; 2 Thess 2:3–8; Rev 13:1–10
Seven-year covenant of peace with Israel	Dan 9:27
Abomination of desolation in Jerusalem	Dan 9:27; 12:11; Matt 24:15–16; Mark 13:14
Great Tribulation	Dan 12:1, 7; Matt 24:21–22; Luke 21:23–25
Mark of the beast	Rev 13:1–10
Outpouring of God's judgments on the earth	Joel 2:11, 31; Rev 15–16
Final military campaign of the antichrist against Israel—Armageddon	Joel 3:9–12; Zech 14:1–3; Rev 16:16; 19:11–21
Mass salvation of Israel at the revelation of Jesus as Messiah (All Israel is saved.)	Zech 12:10–14; Rom 11:26
Return of Messiah Jesus in glory—Parousia	Dan 7:13–14; 1 Thess 4:16–17; Rev 1:7
Resurrection of saints, rapture of living, and return to defeat the antichrist and reign	Matt 24:29–31; 1 Cor 15:51–54; Rev 19
The Millennial Kingdom (1,000-year reign)	Isa 2:2–4; 35:10; Ps 102:20–22; Rev 20

God is wise enough to bring His Redeemer Son into the world, send the gospel to the Gentiles, and bring in their full number so that there will ultimately be people gathered around the throne from every tribe, tongue, and ethnic group. But He has not forgotten His people by covenant, and He will win in the end. He will see the people who once rejected Him finally cry out to Him in belief. Paul described this wisdom of God as "the depths of the riches ... of God! How unsearchable are his judgments and how inscrutable his ways!"[2] *Israel matters theologically as both a sign and a wonder.*

6

WHY ISRAEL MATTERS TO THE CHURCH

Israel is not a side issue for the Church. More and more, the nation and people are coming into focus as the prophetic events are unfolding before our eyes and in our generation. It's time to embrace the implications of Israel and the enduring relevance of her people and Land to redemptive history as well as prophetic promise. That's what this book has been all about.

In the five chapters preceding this one, we have seen evidence of Israel's significance to the Church. We've come to understand the roles the Jewish people and the Land have in our yesterday, our today, and our tomorrow. And we must allow God to shed His love abroad in our hearts for the people, Land, and nation of Israel. As the apostle Paul said, "They are beloved for the sake of their forefathers."[1] And if they're beloved of God—beloved of our Father—then they must be beloved of us.

In Romans 11, the apostle Paul masterfully explained how our futures—the future of the Church and that of Israel—are connected in the purposes and plans of God. Additionally, if it is true that the Church is called to play an important role in the redemptive drama of all Israel, then we must learn:

- What do we do to live in such a way so as to "provoke" Israel to jealousy?
- How should we respond to Israel and the Jewish people?

Checking Our Theology

One of the most important things we must do is become literate in God's purposes for Israel and the Jewish people. If we do not, we will become susceptible to poor theology or indifference toward those who will take centerstage during the end times. We must not allow ourselves to become conceited or deceived, as Paul warned in verses 18 and 25 of Romans 11.

Too many in the Body of Christ have come under the influence of replacement theology that says God has now replaced Israel with the Church. As we discussed in chapter 2, supersessionists allege that the promises made to Abraham are only spiritual and that there is no longer any prophetic significance to Israel after the flesh or the Jewish people. They assert that the regathering of Jews in the Land is mere coincidence and has no bearing on what is taking place in redemptive history. In my opinion, this is a dangerous teaching. It holds the potential of fostering antisemitism, which is borne out by Church history itself.

We must go back to the Word of God to become informed and knowledgeable about Israel and the mystery of God's election of her people. Paul distinctly stated,

For the gifts and the calling of God are irrevocable. For just as you were at one time disobedient to God but now have received mercy because of their disobedience, so they too have now been disobedient in order that by the mercy shown to you they also may now receive mercy. For God has consigned all to disobedience, that he may have mercy on all.

— ROMANS 11:29–32

God has not changed His mind about Israel or His Church. He has elected us all in Christ before the foundation of the world. And He allowed "the partial hardening" to come upon Israel, so the Gentiles could come in, and He is using our receiving mercy as a means to their receiving mercy.[2]

That's the glorious mystery—we as the wild olive shoot have been grafted into the tree, and Israel as the branches that were once cut off will be re-grafted into the same tree!

Interceding for Israel

In light of this mystery, we should want to respond obediently to the call to become intercessors for Israel and the Jewish people. The prophet Isaiah declared, "For Zion's sake I will not keep silent and for Jerusalem's sake I will not be quiet, until her righteousness goes forth as brightness, and her salvation as a burning torch."[3] That's the kind of passionate, persistent intercession God wants the Church to have for Israel. He doesn't want us to remain silent in prayer or petition. He wants us to be like the persistent widow Jesus spoke about in a parable in Luke 18. The widow in that parable repeatedly came before an unjust judge and persistently demanded, "Give me justice against my adversary."[4] The judge finally met her demands, thus illustrating what happens when we "always pray and not lose heart."[5] That's the same insistence and urgency and persistence seen in Isaiah's declaration.

The apostle Paul was heartsick that his kinsmen after the flesh were lost and blinded from the glorious gospel of Jesus Christ. He was so heartsick that he was willing to lose himself if that's what it would take for salvation to reach the Jewish people en mass. He said, "For I could wish that I myself were accursed and cut off from Christ for the sake of my brothers, my kinsmen according to the flesh."[6] This was demonstrated by his consistent attempts to preach in the synagogues even with very little fruit. It is this kind of concern and conviction that will lead us to be intercessors at the end of the age for the Jewish people.

God will use gentile Christians to pray and intercede for the Jewish people in an ironic juxtaposition. Originally, it was to be the Jewish people who would intercede for the nations and bring the light to them. In God's wisdom and manifold glory, He will use those who were not a people, those who were outside the commonwealth of Israel, to pray and bring about the saving grace of Israel in the last hours of human history. He will use the Church as intercessors for Israel and Jerusalem:

> On your walls, O Jerusalem, I have set watchmen; all the day and all the night they shall never be silent. You who put the Lord in remembrance, take no rest, and give him no rest until he establishes Jerusalem and makes it a praise in the earth.

> — ISAIAH 62:6–7

Standing with Israel

We, the Church, must stand with Israel. And the best way to do that is to befriend her. I would encourage friendship. There has been such hostility and separation over the last 2,000 years between followers of Jesus Christ and Jewish people. Friendship and support are vital in this hour to undo the many years of persecution and hatred. It may not be an easy journey, but taking a stance of friendliness and support is the first step toward relationship. This can be as simple as developing a positive attitude toward the Jewish people in general, standing with Israel when the world seems to posture itself against her. Hopefully, you and I can go a step or two farther in meeting and befriending members of the Jewish community for no other reason than to demonstrate that Christians, followers of Yeshua, owe them a debt of gratitude.

With the continuing rise of antisemitism, I have many Jewish friends who have expressed shock and angst about even going out in public during seasons of great turmoil. To know that the Christian community is standing with them may help to disarm and break down the barriers that, for the most part, have been erected by our lack of understanding and the arrogance of wild olive branches relishing our newfound inclusion.

It's time for the Church to pray for Israel. It's time for the Church to love her and her people as God loves her. It's time for the Church to stand with her in her time of need. Why? Because *Israel matters to the Church*—because she matters theologically, politically, historically, today. Israel matters to me, too. More importantly, she matters to God, and now, I hope she matters to you.

TOP 20 QUESTIONS ANSWERED
FOR QUICK REFERENCE

1. Why is Israel significant to Christians?

Israel should be significant to Christians, whether Jewish or Gentile, because Israel is important to God. It is through God's election of the Jewish people that redemption has come into the world, and God is committed to ultimately bringing her back full circle at the end of the age by saving *all Israel*. Paul wrote in Romans 9:3 that he was so grieved over Israel's current state of unbelief that he would rather himself be "accursed." If it weren't for Israel, we Christians would not have the covenants, the Word of God, the patriarchs as our examples, or Jesus Christ, our Lord (see Rom 9:4–5).

Israel should be significant to Christians because part of our responsibility is to prioritize the gospel to go to "the Jew first" (Rom 1:16). This means we should hold a special place in our hearts for the Jewish people and the nation of Israel. We are called to be intercessors for them (see Isa 62). After all, Jesus wept over Jerusalem (see Luke 19:41). He also prayed and prophesied that Jerusalem would one day see Him again when He returns and Jerusalem (Israel) believes in Him (see Matt 23:37–39).

Ultimately, Israel should be significant to Christians because the conflict and the climax of the ages will center around this small but significant nation. The generation to see all of these things take place needs to have a proper biblical perspective of Israel.

2. What is the biblical significance of Israel?

The Bible is an Israel-centric collection of Holy Spirit-inspired writings, meaning that the major story of the Bible is centered around God's covenant relationship with a unique nation, Israel, by and through which a Savior comes and brings salvation to the rest of the world. Because of this, Israel plays a major role in every aspect of the biblical narrative.

3. Why is Israel important to God?

Israel is important to God because of His covenantal faithfulness. God elected Israel to be a nation chosen for His purpose. Why God chose Israel is a mystery hidden within God Himself (see Rom 11:25). This does not mean He loves Israel more than any other nation or people. It means He has bound Himself to this people by a unilateral, unconditional, everlasting covenant.

When God spoke to Abraham in Genesis 12, this became the starting point of God's redemptive plan to redeem humanity and creation. In Genesis 15, God renewed His commitment by entering a covenant with Abraham and making an everlasting promise to him. It would be through the line of Abraham, Isaac, and Jacob (Israel) that the Redeemer would come. Jesus Christ, the Seed of David, is the perfect man and the faithful Israelite whose blood would redeem not just Israel, but all those who believe according to the pattern of Abraham (by faith).

4. Does God still have a special plan for Israel today?

Yes, God's eternal purpose for the Jewish people is still intact. Although the vast majority of Israel and the Jewish people remain in unbelief, God remains faithful. Romans 9–11 details that, although the natural olive branches (Israel) were cut off and currently under judgment because of unbelief, there will come a day when they are grafted back in and *all Israel will be saved.*

5. What does the Bible say about the Land of Israel belonging to the Jewish people? Does Israel have a right to the Land?

God made a unilateral, unconditional, everlasting covenant with Abraham and declared that the land of Canaan would be "an everlasting possession" to all of Abraham's descendants through Isaac (see Gen 17:7–8; 21:12; Rom 9:7; Heb 11:18). This promise was fulfilled in part but not fully with the boundaries that God gave to Abraham. The fullness of this promise will take place under the leadership of Jesus the Messiah during the Millennial Kingdom.

6. Why is Jerusalem important to Christians?

Jerusalem is important to Christians for many reasons. First, it is the birthplace of the Church. God poured out His Spirit upon the first members of His Church on Pentecost Sunday in Acts 2. This was in fulfillment of the prophecy given by Joel (see Joel 2:28–29).

Jerusalem is also important to Christians because it was the starting point for the Great Commission as given by Jesus. He said, "And you will be my witnesses in Jerusalem and in Judea and Samaria, and to the end of the earth" (Acts 1:8).

Ultimately, Jerusalem is important to Christians because Jesus promised that He would return a second time to Jerusalem (see Matt 23:39). The Bible makes it clear that, when Jesus returns, He will reign upon the throne of His father David, for 1,000 years (see Luke 1:32; Rev 20:6). The Bible describes that, in the regeneration, there will be a new Jerusalem that comes down from Heaven (see Rev 21:2–4).

7. What is the significance of the Temple Mount in Jerusalem to Christians?

The **Temple Mount** is significant because it is the location of the Temple that Solomon built and was later rebuilt under Zerubbabel. After it was destroyed by the Romans in AD 70, it lay in ruins until Muslim invaders built the **Dome of the Rock** and the **Al Aqsa Mosque** several hundred years later.

Currently, it is the most contested piece of real estate in the world because of the global/political and spiritual implications. Faithful Jews are still anticipating the arrival of Messiah and the rebuilding of the Third Temple. Christians who know and believe that Jesus Christ is the Messiah see Temple Mount as still significant, not because a Third Temple is necessary to worship God, but in anticipation of the arrival of the man of lawlessness, the antichrist. Jesus quoted Daniel's prophecy about this figure making an abomination of desolation of the Holy of Holies at the middle point of the tribulation. Paul also made reference to this event as a major sign of the end of the age (see Dan 9:27; Matt 24:15–16; 2 Thess 2:1–4).

8. What is replacement theology, and what's wrong with it?

In short, replacement theology (supersessionism) is the theological premise that all of the covenant promises made to natural Israel and the Jewish people have now been redirected to the Church. It asserts that God has officially divorced natural Israel and cut her off permanently, and she is and will continue to be under the judgment of God because of her unbelief and rejection of the Messiah. The Church, made up of Gentiles and Jews, is seen by supersessionists as now the Israel of God. Because of this, the Land promises and prophecies of a return to the Land and future revival of the Jewish people before the end of the age are rejected. Current national Israel is seen to have no prophetic significance or fulfillment.

This theological approach developed in the early stages of the Church as it grew more Gentile-centric has led to the hostility and persecution of Jews by Christian institutions throughout the last two millennia. It has also hindered the Church from bringing the gospel *first* to the Jews as Paul said in Romans 1:16.

9. How should Christians view Israel in relation to Bible prophecy?

Christians must recognize the ongoing importance of Israel when it comes to where Bible prophecy is heading. We have too much tendency in Western civilization to think that all things revolve around us. Bible prophecy is not Euro-centric or American-centric; it is Israel-centric. The Bible makes it clear that Jesus will return to Jerusalem, there will be a seven-year covenant that the antichrist will establish with Israel, and the abomination of desolation will trigger the last three-and-a-half years of the tribulation, which will take place in Israel. All nations of the earth will hate the Jewish people, and confederations of nations will form to destroy them. God's wrath will be unleashed upon those nations in defense of Israel.

As prophecy continues to unfold within immediate history, an understanding of Israel's central role leading up to the return of Jesus will be vital for believers in order for us to avoid deception and offense. Otherwise, we will be vulnerable to not understanding what is taking place and succumbing to offense and the same spirit of delusion that is coming upon the earth (see Ps 2; Dan 9:27; Zech 12:3; 2 Thess 2:1–12).

10. What role does Israel play in the end times according to the Bible?

Israel will play a central role in the events at the end of the age. It was a prophetic necessity for Jews to return to the Land and for Israel to be restored before the return of Jesus. With Israel being reborn as a nation and the city of Jerusalem coming back into Jewish control during the Six-Day War in 1967, the prophetic time clock has restarted, awaiting the final events of prophecy to be fulfilled. Jesus said Himself in Luke 13:34–35:

> O Jerusalem, Jerusalem, the city that kills the prophets and stones those who are sent to it! How often would I have gathered your children together as a hen gathers her brood under her wings, and you were not willing! Behold, your house is forsaken. And I tell you, you will not see me until you say, "Blessed is he who comes in the name of the Lord!"

The implications of this statement (and others) is that Jesus, the Jewish Messiah, will return to Jerusalem occupied and under the dominance of Jewish people who are expecting and welcoming Him finally as the King of Israel.

11. Is the establishment of modern Israel a fulfillment of biblical prophecy?

Yes, for several reasons. First, God Himself made an everlasting covenant with Abraham and His descendants, Isaac and Jacob (Israel). It involved the land of Canaan (Israel) as "an everlasting possession" (Gen 17:7–8). This means that God is committed to seeing His purposes and promises to Israel ultimately fulfilled, regardless of Israel's initiative. It's important to realize that this covenant is not due to Israel's merit or goodness, but is based upon God's divine election and calling for His own purposes.

Secondly, it is obvious that the current modern State is the *beginning* of the return to the Land. Even though the current modern State of Israel is a mixture of secular and religious cultures, it has precipitated the first major return of Jewish exiles from the nations back into the Land. This return is in large part still a return in unbelief. For many who have made aliyah, it is an expression of pursuit to know and serve the God of Abraham, Isaac, and Jacob.

Within Israel today, there is a growing anticipation and expectation for the coming of Messiah. This is part of the end-time prophetic playbook in which the antichrist will emerge at a time of crisis and appear to be a kind of savior or messianic figure. The Bible talks about a *second return* that will take place at a time when the Jewish people finally receive and acknowl-edge Yeshua (Jesus) as Messiah during the last stages of this present age.

12. What is Christian Zionism, and is it biblical?

David Pawson, the renowned British author, defined Christian Zionism as

> a movement among Gentile Believers in the Jewish Messiah to advocate and support the Jewish return to their own land, convinced that they still have a God-given right to be there and, indeed, that he would bring and has brought them home again, thus keeping his promises recorded in scriptures.[1]

To believe in the literal fulfillment of God's covenant promises to Abraham and his descendants in the spirit by faith as well as the natural descendants of Israel necessarily requires one to be a Christian Zionist. This does not mean that we blindly support every political decision or cultural reality in the modern State of Israel. It also does not mean that we assume that Jewish people are saved outside the shed blood of Jesus, through His New (renewed) Covenant. It simply means we recognize that God is still working within redemptive history to restore, reveal, and redeem Israel after the flesh.

13. Do Christians believe that Jews need to convert to Christianity to be saved?

The Bible makes it clear that there is no salvation for anyone outside the sacrificial and atoning death and resurrection of Jesus Christ. We must acknowledge Him as Savior and Messiah, and turn from our sins and all other dead works.

The apostle Peter stood up and preached to the inhabitants of Jerusalem and Jews who had gathered on pilgrimage to celebrate Pentecost, and he called them to repent and believe. He did not affirm that they were saved by some separate means than the Gentiles. He called them to acknowledge that the One who had been crucified was indeed their long-awaited Messiah. He said, "And there is salvation in no one else, for there is no other name under heaven given among men by which we must be saved" (Acts 4:12).

For many Jewish people considering Jesus, the word *convert* or *converting* is a painful word that conjures up memories of forced conversions throughout history. For many, it feels that to become a Christian or even to confess that Jesus is Lord (i.e., Yeshua is Messiah) is to betray their heritage and the faith of their forefathers. It may be better to understand that Jewish believers are not leaving their Jewish roots or heritage behind but actually coming into the fullness and fulfillment of what it means to be a Jew. Some prefer the phrase *completed Jew*.

Regardless of how it is described, there is no other means of salvation than through the grace of God and faith in His Son Jesus.

14. Isn't Israel an apartheid state?

Israel is the furthest thing from an apartheid state. Made up of 10 million residents, 73 percent of the population is Jewish.[2] About 21 percent is of Arab descent, and 5 percent is classified as "other."[3] All of these groups have full citizenship and rights. Arabs and others are elected to the Knesset, serve as judges, and own businesses and property. *Apartheid* is a system of keeping groups separate, often according to race and ethnicity, and treating them differently, especially when this results in the disadvantage of a primary group. This is not the case in Israel although it has been parroted by antisemitic groups and anti-Zionist propaganda.

The other Middle Eastern nations surrounding Israel have almost no Jewish presence in them, and for the most part, the Jews in these other Middle Eastern nations have been pushed out by persecution or legal decree.

15. Didn't Israel take the Land away from the Palestinian people?

The history of the displacement of what is now called the Palestinian people is complicated. Originally, anyone who lived in the territory known today as Jordan, Israel, and Gaza —Jew and Arab alike—were referred to as *Palestinians*. This was never a sovereign nation. It was a territory that had been subjugated by stronger empires. For several centuries, the

Ottoman Empire controlled the Land called Palestine and allowed Jews, Arabs, and other ethnicities to live there and work the Land for their Syrian owners. When Israel reconstituted in her ancient homeland and in 1948 established the modern State of Israel, many Arabs and other non-Jewish inhabitants were encouraged by Israel's enemies to leave the Land temporarily until they could wipe out the Jews once and for all, and then they could return to reclaim what was theirs and what had been gained from the Jewish defeat. When Israel prevailed, many were displaced. The leaders of those nations, like Egypt, who had encouraged Jews to get out of the crossfire temporarily, were not willing to bring Jews into their fold and grant Jews citizenship.

It's also important to know that from the last half of the nineteenth century until 1948, Jewish exiles upon returning to the Land invested their fortunes to build cities and the infrastructure of what is now Israel. They drained swamps, established farms, and built modern cities like Tel Aviv. There was a firmly established culture flourishing long before 1948.

16. Didn't God divorce Israel for her unbelief?

In the Old Testament, God portrayed His relationship with Israel as a marriage. He often addressed Israel through the prophets as an unfaithful wife, who pursued idols and false gods like other lovers. In Jeremiah 3:1, God said, "You have played the whore with many lovers; and would you return to me? declares the Lord." He went further and stated that, because of Israel's unfaithfulness, He would divorce her and put her away permanently.

> And I thought, "After she has done all this she will return to me," but she did not return, and her treacherous sister Judah saw it. She saw that for all the adulteries of that faithless one, Israel, I had sent her away with a decree of divorce.
>
> — JEREMIAH 3:7–8

Although God was expressing His anger and frustration with Israel's unfaithfulness, just a few verses later, He beckoned her to return to Him once again.

> Return, faithless Israel, declares the Lord. I will not look on you in anger, for I am merciful, declares the Lord; I will not be angry forever. Only acknowledge your guilt, that you rebelled against the Lord your God.
>
> — JEREMIAH 3:12–13

Even though God had every right to divorce Israel, He has demonstrated His unwavering love and covenant faithfulness to her by wooing her and pursuing her until she at once returns to faithfulness. God promised that He will never divorce her or forget her—that He will win out in the end:

> Thus says the Lord, who gives the sun for light by day and the fixed order of the moon and the stars for light by night, who stirs up the sea so that its waves roar— the Lord of hosts is his name: If this fixed order departs from before me, declares the Lord, then shall the offspring of Israel cease from being a nation before me

forever. Thus says the Lord: If the heavens above can be measured, and the foundations of the earth below can be explored, then I will cast off all the offspring of Israel for all that they have done, declares the Lord.

— JEREMIAH 31:35–37

17. Should Christians support efforts to rebuild the Jewish Temple in Jerusalem?

While students of the Bible understand that a future Third Temple is described in Bible prophecy, it is important to be reminded that this is only because the Jewish people in large part still do not acknowledge that One greater than the Temple has already come (see Matt 12:6).

God has no obligation to fill this new Temple built with hands with His Presence, since now He dwells within His people who are the temple of the Holy Spirit. The sacrifices that would be performed in such a new Temple are not valid. This new Temple plays a part in the redemptive history of Israel and its outworking at the end of the age, but Christians are not called to do anything other than be aware of the Third Temple's significance when its building does take place.

18. How should Christians view the conflict between Israel and Palestine?

It is vital for Christians to view the ongoing conflict between Israel and the Palestinians with clear eyes. On one hand, we must acknowledge Israel's existential right to exist, her political legitimacy, and her right to defend herself against those who have publicly called for her annihilation. On the other hand, it is important to recognize that there are innocent people caught in the crossfire of this conflict in Palestinian-controlled territories who need our prayers and support as well. Jesus commended the peacemakers. In a fallen, war-torn world, we should aspire and pray for peace, love all people whom Jesus shed His precious blood to redeem, and acknowledge that, in the midst of very complicated circumstances, there will be tragedies.

Being sober-minded and educated about the history of the conflict, the powers and authorities at work, and the prophetic nature of this conflict will allow us to show support for Israel and also pray for God's Kingdom of peace to fully come.

19. Is the Church now the Israel of God?

This is a commonly held belief based upon a single passage that, in my opinion, is interpreted wrongly. In Galatians 6:16, the apostle Paul signed off his letter with this statement, "And as for all who walk by this rule, peace and mercy be upon them, and upon the Israel of God."

Because Paul addressed the Church (or churches) in the region of Galatia, it is assumed that he was attributing this statement to the Church. It is more likely that Paul was including in his letter those who were believing Jews who were now part of the Church. Regardless of whether this is the correct interpretation or not, what is clear from the rest of the New Testament and especially Paul's letters is that he always made a distinction between Israel according to the flesh, his countrymen, and the Church that included Jews and Gentiles alike. Nowhere, including here in this verse, did Paul ever call the Church *Israel*.

20. Didn't Jesus say that He was taking the Kingdom away from Israel and giving it to others because of her wickedness?

The short answer is no. Jesus taught a parable in Matthew 21 about a vineyard owner who leased out his land to tenants:

> "There was a master of a house who planted a vineyard and put a fence around it and dug a winepress in it and built a tower and leased it to tenants, and went into another country. When the season for fruit drew near, he sent his servants to the tenants to get his fruit. And the tenants took his servants and beat one, killed another, and stoned another. Again he sent other servants, more than the first. And they did the same to them. Finally he sent his son to them, saying, 'They will respect my son.' But when the tenants saw the son, they said to themselves, 'This is the heir. Come, let us kill him and have his inheritance.' And they took him and threw him out of the vineyard and killed him. When therefore the owner of the vineyard comes, what will he do to those tenants?" They said to him, "He will put those wretches to a miserable death and let out the vineyard to other tenants who will give him the fruits in their seasons."
>
> — MATTHEW 21:33–41

In this parable, the tenants who come under scrutiny were not all of Israel. The tenants were the religious leaders of the people of Israel—the leaders who knowingly rejected Jesus.

When Jesus went to build His Church, He began with 12 Jewish apostles as the foundation. This is what is meant by "other tenants" or other leaders. This parable in no way means that God has decided to rescind the Land promises or the commitment to graft back in the natural branches (i.e., Israel/Jews) before the end of this age.

RECOMMENDED BOOKS
FOR FURTHER STUDY

David Baron, *Israel in the Plan of God,* (Grand Rapids, MI: Kregel Classics, 2000).

David Baron, *The Jewish Problem: It's Solution: Or, Israel's Present and Future,* (Lawton, OK: Trumpet Press, 2019).

Avner Boskey, *Jews, Arabs, & the Middle East: A Messianic Perspective,* (Nashville: David's Tent Publishing, 2017).

Eric H. Cline, *1177 B.C.: The Year Civilization Collapsed,* (Princeton, NJ: Princeton University Press, 2014).

Eric H. Cline, *After 1177 B.C.: The Survival of Civilizations,* (Princeton, NJ: Princeton University Press, 2024).

Alan Dershowitz, *War Against the Jews: How to End Hamas Barbarism,* (New York: Hot Books, 2023).

Alan Dershowitz, *The Case for Israel,* (Nashville: Trade Paper Press, 2003).

Daniel Gordis, *Israel: A Concise History of a Nation Reborn,* (Israel: Ecco, 2016).

Theodor Herzl, *The Jewish State,* (New York: Skyhorse Publishing, 2019).

Walter C. Kaiser, Jr., *Jewish Christianity: Why Believing Jews and Gentiles Parted Ways in the Early Church,* (Lampion House Publishing, LLC, 2020).

Walter C. Kaiser, Jr., *A History of Israel: From the Bronze Age through the Jewish Wars,* (Nashville: B&H Academic, 2016).

Titus Kennedy, *The Essential Archaeological Guide to Bible Lands: Uncovering Biblical Sites of the Ancient Near East and Mediterranean World,* (Eugene, OR: Harvest House Publishers, 2023).

Titus Kennedy, *Unearthing the Bible: 101 Archaeological Discoveries That Bring the Bible to Life,* (Eugene, OR: Harvest House Publishers, 2020).

David Pawson, *Defending Christian Zionism,* (Travelers Rest, SC: True Potential, Inc., 2008).

Douglas Petrovich, *Origins of the Hebrews: New Evidence of Israelites in Egypt from Joseph to the Exodus,* (Nashville: New Creation, 2021).

Joel Richardson, *Sinai to Zion: The Untold Story of the Triumphant Return of Jesus,* (Leawood, KS: Winepress Media, 2020).

Joel Richardson, *When a Jew Rules the World: What the Bible Really Says About Israel in the Plan of God,* (Leawood, KS: Winepress Media, 2015).

Adolph Saphir, *Christ & Israel: Lectures on the Jews,* ed. David Baron, (FAI Publishing, 2021).

Adolph Saphir, *The Jews As Custodians And Witnesses,* (Whitefish, MT: Kissinger Publishing, 2010).

Daniel Sokatch, *Can We Talk About Israel? A Guide for the Curious, Confused, and Conflicted,* (New York: Bloomsbury Publishing, 2022).

Michael J. Vlach, *Has the Church Replaced Israel? A Theological Evaluation,* (Nashville: B&H Publishing Group, 2010).

John H. Walton, *Chronological and Background Charts of the Old Testament* (Zondervan Charts), (Grand Rapids, MI: Zondervan Academic, 1994).

GLOSSARY
IMPORTANT TERMS, ORGANIZATIONS & PEOPLE

Abbas, Mahmoud (1935–): is the current head of the Fatah party, chairman of the Palestine Liberation Organization (PLO), and president of the Palestinian Authority (PA).

Al Aqsa Mosque: is the second oldest mosque in Islam, is one of three of the holiest sites in Islam, and is located on the Temple Mount in the Old City of Jerusalem.

aliyah: means "ascent" in Hebrew and refers to Jewish immigration from the diaspora to Palestine region (pre-State) and Israel. The First Aliyah occurred before political Zionism in the late 1800s, and aliyahs continue to the present day.

antisemitism: refers to "a certain perception of Jews, which may be expressed as hatred toward Jews. Rhetorical and physical manifestations of antisemitism are directed toward Jewish or non-Jewish individuals and their property, toward Jewish community institutions and religious facilities."[1] (A hyphen isn't employed as "a hyphened 'anti-Semitism' gave credence to Nazi racial theories, wherein humanity was divided into superior and inferior subcategories.")[2]

Arab League: was established in Cairo, Egypt, in March of 1945 to represent the Arab States. The initial members included Egypt, Iraq, Lebanon, North Yemen, Saudi Arabia, Syria, and Transjordan. As of this publishing, the league has 22 members.

Arafat, Yasser (1929–2004): was the chairman of the Palestine Liberation Organization (PLO) from 1969 to 2004 and the president of the Palestinian Authority from 1994 to 2004.

Arch of Titus: is a honorific arch near the Roman Forum. Emperor Domitian, the younger brother of Titus, built it c. AD 81 "to commemorate Titus's official deification . . . and the victory of Titus together with their father, Vespasian, over the Jewish rebellion in Judaea."[3]

Ashkenazi(c) Jews: from the Hebrew word *Ashkenaz*, referring to Germany, these are Jews who are from France, Germany, and Eastern Europe. It includes their descendants as well. "Most American Jews today are Ashkenazim [plural], descended from Jews who emigrated from Germany and Eastern Europe from the mid 1800s to the early 1900s."[4]

Barak, Ehud (1942–): served as the ninth prime minister of Israel from 1999 to 2001. He was the leader of the Labor Party twice—the first time serving 1997–2001 and the second 2007–2011.

Bar Kokhba Revolt (AD 132–136): was a failed Jewish rebellion against Roman rule in Judaea. It was led by a messianic figure called Simon Bar Kokhba (a name given him, meaning "Son of a Star"). After "an abortive attempt to rebuild the Jerusalem Temple, . . . Hadrian founded a city of his own in Jerusalem called Aelia Capitolina, where he erected a temple to the Greek god Zeus. It is probable that Hadrian prohibited circumcision even before the Bar Kokhba Revolt.... It was in this context, as well as on the basis of the strong messianic yearnings ... that some elements in the Jewish population of Palestine began preparing for revolt in the 120s."[5]

Ben-Gurion, David (1886–1973): was the national founder of the State of Israel in 1948. He was the first signer of the Israeli Declaration of Independence as well as one the individuals to produce its final text. He was the first prime minister for the nation (1955–1963).

British Mandate (1920): as assigned by the League of Nations at the San Remo conference, gave the administration of Palestine and Transjordan—both having formerly been part of the Ottoman Empire—to Britain. (France was given oversight of Syria and Lebanon.)

Camp David Summit (July 11–24, 2000): was a meeting held at the US presidential retreat in Camp David, Maryland, for the purpose of negotiating a final settlement to the Israeli-Palestinian conflict in accordance with the 1993 Oslo Agreement. It was attended by Israeli Prime Minister Ehud Barak, PA Chairman Yasser Arafat, and President Bill Clinton. The parties present did not come to any agreement.

Dead Sea Scrolls: are ancient Jewish manuscripts discovered over the course of several years (1947–1956) at the Qumran Caves on the northern shore of the Dead Sea in the West Bank. One of the more important finds of modern archaeology.

diaspora: is the exile or dispersion of Jews out of their ancestral homeland and their settling in other nations around the world.

Dome of the Rock: is an Islamic shrine at the center of the Al Aqsa Mosque buildings on the Temple Mount in the Old City of Jerusalem.

Druze: is a religious and political group that broke away from the Ismaili Muslims in the eleventh century. Regarded by the larger Muslim community as heretical, they live predominantly in Lebanon and Syria.

"From the river to the sea, Palestine shall be free!" is chanted in pro-Palestinian rallies around the world. It is a call for the establishment of a State of Palestine from the Jordan River to the Mediterranean Sea and for the eradication of Israel.

Gallant, Yoav (1958–): serves as the Minister of Defense for Israel since 2022. He is a former commander of the Southern Command in the IDF. He is a member of the Likud Party.

Gaza: is one of two Palestinian territories. (The West Bank is the other, though Gaza is the smallest.) It is bordered by Israel on the east and north, Egypt on the southwest, and the

Mediterranean Sea on the west. Its de facto government is Hamas.

genocide: combined from the Greek prefix *genus,* meaning "race" or "tribe," and the Latin suffix, *cide*, meaning "killing," it refers to the intentional killing of people from a particular nation or ethnic group in order to completely destroy that nation or group.

Golan Heights: is a hilly region that overlooks the upper Jordan River valley on the west and was unilaterally annexed by Israel in 1981. Lebanon is to its north, Syria to its east, and Jordan to its south. It was named after the biblical city of refuge, Golan, in Bashan.

Hamas: is an acronym for **Harakat al-Muqawama al-Islamiya,** meaning Islamic Resistance Movement. During the first Palestinian intifada, it emerged in the late 1980s, "publish[ing] its charter in 1988, calling for the murder of Jews, the destruction of Israel, and in Israel's place, the establishment of an Islamic society in historic Palestine."[6] It has been the de facto governing body in the Gaza Strip since 2006. The US designated Hamas as a Foreign Terrorist Organization in 1997. Argentina, Australia, Canada, Israel, Japan, Paraguay, New Zealand, the United Kingdom, and the European Union have since also designated Hamas as a terrorist organization. The UN Security Council has not placed Hamas on its list of terrorist organizations as of the date of publication of this book.

Herzl, Theodor (1860–1904): is often called the Visionary of the State of Israel. He authored *A Jewish State* in 1896 and convened the First Zionist Congress in Basel, Switzerland, in 1897, forming the Zionist Organization to promote Jewish immigration to Palestine to form a Jewish state.

Hezbollah: is a Shiite Muslim political party and militant group based in Lebanon. "Founded in the chaos of the fifteen-year Lebanese Civil War, the Iran-backed group is driven by its opposition to Israel and its resistance to Western influence in the Middle East."[7] It has actively carried out international terrorist attacks and "has been designated a terrorist organization by the United States and many other countries, though some just apply this label to its armed wing."[8]

historicity: is the historical actuality of people and events as opposed to the story of myth or legend.

Holocaust (1933–1945): "was the systematic, state-sponsored persecution and murder of six million European Jews by the Nazi German regime and its allies and collaborators."[9]

Houthis: are a US designated terrorist group located in Yemen and act as an Iranian proxy. "The Houthis' infamous, Iranian-inspired rallying cry points to their ambitions beyond Yemen: 'God is great, death to America, death to Israel, a curse upon the Jews, victory to Islam.'"[10]

International Criminal Court (ICC): is an intergovernmental organization and international tribunal seated in The Hague, Netherlands, founded on July 1, 2002, in Rome, Italy, that investigates, prosecutes, and tries individuals accused of war crimes, genocide, and crimes against humanity. It should not be confused with the International Court of Justice (ICJ), which is one of the organs of the UN.

Intifada: is an Arabic word literally meaning "shaking off," and can refer to two specific violent uprisings of Palestinians in the West Bank and Gaza Strip aimed to put an end to Israel's occupation of these territories. The First Intifada began in December of 1987 and the second in September 2000. However, the term is now being used in a more general sense as any uprising against or violence against Israel. "The phrase 'Globalize the Intifada' calls for people from around the globe to participate in rising up against Israel."[11]

Islamic jihadi terrorist group: refers to any militant Islamic movement that carries out religious violence against individuals, governments, or people.

Islamic Republic of Iran: known as Persia until 1935, became an Islamic republic in 1979 after overthrowing the ruling monarchy and Shah Mohammad Reza Pahlavi, who was forced into exile. Located in southwestern Asia, it is led by a supreme leader who as the head of state holds the highest political and religious authority.

Israel Defense Forces (IDF): was formed in 1948 and operates as a conscript military with both men and women serving together. It is comprised of Israeli Ground Forces, Israeli Air Force, and Israeli Navy.

Kitos War (AD 115–117): broke out as the Jews of Cyrene

revolted against Roman rule. Lukas (or Andreas as he was also known) led the revolt, seizing control in Cyrenaica. Jews also revolted in Egypt, Mesopotamia, Judaea, and Cyprus during the war. Though the war resulted in much death and destruction by the Jews, it was finally suppressed my the Romans in 117.[12]

Knesset: is the unicameral parliament of Israel and is the supreme authority of the State.

Luther, Martin (1483–1546): was a German priest, theologian, author of *Ninety-five Theses,* and often called father of Protestantism. A few years before his death, he wrote an antisemitic treatise titled *On the Jews and Their Lies*.

Mizrahi(c) Jews: from the Hebrew word meaning "Eastern," these are a subdivision of Sephardic Jews and are specifically from Northern Africa and the Middle East. "In Israel today, a little more than half of all Jews are Mizrachim, descended from Jews who have been in the Land since ancient times or who were forced out of Arab countries after Israel was founded."[13]

Mosaic covenant: was unlike the Abrahamic covenant in that it was a bilateral covenant, a two-sided agreement. There were requirements that Israel had to meet in the Mosaic covenant in order for her to receive the promises of this covenant. Though coming 430 years after the Abrahamic covenant, it did not replace that first covenant.

Nasser, Gamal (1918–1970): named himself the Egyptian prime minister (1954–1956) and took control as president (1956–1970) after decreeing a constitution that set Egypt up as a socialist Arab state with one political party and an official religion (Islam).

Netanyahu, Benjamin "Bibi" (1949–): is the ninth prime minister of Israel and is the longest-serving prime minister in Israel's history. He chairs the Likud Party that was founded in 1973 by Menachem Begin and Ariel Sharon.

Palestine: is the pejorative name the ancient Romans gave to the Land of Israel. More specifically, "the Romans renamed the province Syria Palaestina—that is, 'Palestinian Syria.' They did so resentfully, as a punishment, to obliterate the link between the Jews (in Hebrew, Y'hudim and in Latin Judaei) and the province (the Hebrew name of which was Y'hudah). 'Palaestina referred to the Philistines, whose home base had been on the Mediterranean coast."[14] In the more recent past, Palestine has referred to the geographic region in the Middle East that includes present-day Israel, the West Bank, and the Gaza Strip. Today, Palestine refers to the territories of the West Bank and Gaza.

Palestine Liberation Organization (PLO): is internationally recognized as the official representative of the Palestinian people. It was founded in 1964 and is headquartered in the West Bank.

Palestinian Authority (PA): is officially known as the Palestinian National Authority. It was formed in 1994 and exercises partial civil oversight of Palestinian enclaves in the West Bank.

Peel Commission: formally known as the Palestinian Royal Commission, was headed by and named after Lord Robert Peel. The commission was an inquiry into the roots of the Arab-Jewish conflict.

Popular Front for the Liberation of Palestine (PFLP): is considered a terrorist group based in Gaza and the West Bank. Combining nationalism with Marxist-Leninist ideology, it views "the destruction of Israel as integral to the struggle to remove Western capitalism from the Middle East and ultimately establish a Communist Palestinian state with Jerusalem as its capital." [15]

Second Intifada: was the second major uprising (intifada) of Palestinians against Israeli occupation. It began in 2000 and was suppressed in 2005.

Sephardic Jews: from the Hebrew word *Sepharad,* these are Jews of Spain, Portugal, North Africa, and the Middle East, including their descendants. "Most of the early Jewish settlers of North America were Sephardic. The first Jewish congregation in North America, Shearith Israel, founded in what is now New York in 1684, was Sephardic and is still active." [16]

Sinai Peninsula: lies between the Gulf of Suez and the Suez Canal on the west and the Gulf of Aqaba and the Negev on the east. The Mediterranean Sea is to its north and the Red Sea to the south. The peninsula connects Africa with Asia, and it was occupied by Israeli forces during the Six-Day War.

Six-Day War (June 5–10, 1967): was a brief war between Israel and the Arab States of Egypt, Syria, and Jordan. It was won by Israel and resulted in the Israeli occupation of the West Bank and Gaza.

sovereign state: is an independent state with absolute power over a particular territory. It has a permanent population, defined territory, a government not under another, and an ability to interact with other states.[17]

supersessionism: commonly known as *replacement theology,* is a Christian belief that the Christian Church has superseded or replaced Israel as the people of God. In its most radical form, it espouses the belief that "Israel's lack of faithfulness was so persistent that eventually the Lord permanently stripped her of the unique calling and election that she held throughout the Old Testament period."[18]

Table of Nations: is also known as the Generations of Noah because it is the genealogy of the sons of Noah according to the Bible, as well as the dispersion through the earth after the flood.

Tell el-Amarna Tablets: are several hundred clay tablets discovered in Tel el-Amarna, dating to the fourteenth century BC, that are diplomatic correspondence between Egypt and representatives in Canaan.

Temple Mount: is the hotly contested site in the Old City of Jerusalem. It's the holiest site in Judaism because it's where both the First and Second Temples once stood. "To Christians, it was the place where Jesus preached against corruption in the Temple and expelled moneychangers. To Muslims, the Temple Mount's sanctity would stem from the Al Aqsa Mosque and the Dome of the Rock ... from which Muslim tradition asserts that Mohammed ascended to heaven."[19]

Titus (AD 39–81): was the Roman emperor from AD 79 to 81, succeeding his father Vespasian as emperor. In AD 70, Titus sent his troops throughout Jerusalem, killing its citizens, tearing down all the city walls except what is now known as the Wailing Wall, and setting the city ablaze.

West Bank: is one of two Palestinian territories. (Gaza is the other.) It is landlocked near the coast of the Mediterranean Sea and is bordered by Jordan and the Dead Sea to the east, and Israel to the north, west, and south. Israel occupies the West Bank but has not annexed it. There are Israeli settlements in the West Bank, but they are not under Israeli sovereignty.

World Zionist Organization (WZO): is a non-governmental organization promoting Zionism. Originally called the Zionist Organization and renamed in 1960, it was founded by Theodor Herzl at the First Zionist Congress in 1897.

Zionism: refers to both a belief as well as a movement. As a belief, it affirms Jews are a national community and have a right as Jews to their ancestral homeland. As a movement, it called for the self-determination and statehood for the Jewish people in Israel, and that goal was achieved on May 14, 1948. Zionism continues to find expression in the development and protection of the Jewish nation in her homeland.

NOTES

1. Why Israel Matters to Me

1. See Ps 48:2; Jer 3:18; Zech 8:3; Matt 5:35; Rev 3:12.
2. See Isa 62:7.

2. Why Israel Matters Today

1. Jewish News Syndicate, "Full text of Netanyahu's speech to joint session of Congress," *JNS,* July 24, 2024, https://www.jns.org/full-text-of-netanyahus-speech-to-joint-session-of-congress/ (accessed July 25, 2024).
2. "Israel-Hamas War: What You Need To Know," *American Jewish Committee,* https://www.ajc.org/IsraelHamasWar/ (accessed May 31, 2024).
3. Wikipedia contributors, "Israel–Hamas war hostage crisis," *Wikipedia, The Free Encyclopedia,* https://en.wikipedia.org/w/index.php?title=Israel%E2%80%93Hamas_war_hostage_crisis&oldid=1226157159/(accessed June 2, 2024).
4. JTA, "Was Hamas's attack on Saturday the bloodiest day for Jews since the Holocaust?" *The Times of Israel,* Oct 9, 2023, https://www.timesofisrael.com/was-hamass-attack-on-saturday-the-bloodiest-day-for-jews-since-the-holocaust/ (accessed on August 1, 2024).
5. Betsy Reed, "About 100,000 turn out in London for pro-Palestine rally," *The Guardian,* https://www.theguardian.com/world/2023/oct/21/about-100000-turn-out-in-london-for-pro-palestine-rally/ (accessed June 1, 2024).
6. JP Staff, "Israel's population closing in on 10 million in 2024 demographic update," *The Jerusalem Post,* Feb 11, 2024, 10:28 a.m., https://www.jpost.com/israel-news/article-786265#google_vignette/ (accessed June 2, 2024).
7. Madeline Coggins, "Students blast colleges for anti-Israel protests: 'It's diversity, equity and inclusion except for the Jews,'" *FoxBusiness,* https://www.foxbusiness.com/politics/students-blast-colleges-anti-israel-protests-diversity-equity-inclusion-except-jews/ (accessed June 2, 2024).
8. Stefanie Dazio, "USC's move to cancel commencement amid protests draws criticism from students, alumni," *AP,* April 25, 2024, https://apnews.com/article/israel-palestine-war-campus-protests-usc-cff0c1e59fc6164f615a2686d7f1b401/ (accessed July 1, 2024).

9. United Nations Meetings Coverage and Press Releases, "General Assembly Adopts Resolution Calling for Immediate, Sustained Humanitarian Truce Leading to Cessation of Hostilities between Israel, Hamas," GA/12548, *United Nations,* Oct 27 2023, https://press.un.org/en/2023/ga12548.doc.htm/ (accessed June 2, 2024).

10. Lisa Schlein, "UN rights council accuses Israel of war crimes against Palestinians," *Voice of America,* April 5, 2024, 2:55 p.m., https://www.voanews.com/a/un-rights-council-accuses-israel-of-war-crimes-against-palestinians/7558605.html/ (accessed May 31, 2024).

11. Anti-Defamation League, "Hamas in Its Own Words," *ADL,* Jan 10, 2024, https://www.adl.org/resources/blog/hamas-its-own-words/ (accessed July 23, 2024).

12. David Roach, "Most US Pastors Speak Out in Response to George Floyd's Death," *Christianity Today,* June 16, 2020, https://www.christianitytoday.com/news/2020/june/pastors-george-floyd-racism-church-barna-research.html/ (accessed June 2, 2024).

13. Gary Burge, *Jesus and the Land: The New Testament Challenge to "Holy Land" Theology,* (United Kingdom: Baker Publishing Group, 2010), 86.

14. Mike Vlach, "Does Romans 4:13 Universalize Israel's Land Promises?" *Christian Worldview and Theology,* March 8, 2017, https://mikevlach.blogspot.com/search?q=Romans+4%3A13/ (accessed November 14, 2024).

15. Joel Richardson, *When a Jew Rules the World: What the Bible Really Says about Israel in the Plan of God,* (Leawood, KS: Winepress, 2015), 17.

16. Michael J. Vlach, *Has the Church Replaced Israel? A Theological Evaluation,* (Nashville: B&H Publishing Group, 2010), 97–98.

17. Joel Richardson, *When a Jew Rules the World,* 19.

18. Ibid, 4–5.

19. See Jer 3:17; Zech 14; Rev 14:1–4.

20. Efrat Forster, "Making aliyah to a nation at war: Jews worldwide rediscover Israel following Oct. 7 tragedy," *Israel Hayom,* January 19, 2024, https://www.israelhayom.com/2024/01/19/making-aliyah-to-a-nation-at-war-jews-worldwide-rediscover-israel-following-oct-7-tragedy/ (accessed July 26, 2024).

21. Ibid.

22. Ibid.

23. AP, "Israel's anthem jeered, players booed during Paris Olympics soccer opener against Mali amid heavy police presence," *ABC News Australia,* https://www.abc.net.au/news/2024-07-25/paris-olympic-games-israel-soccer-team-anthem-boos/104140216#/ (accessed on July 24, 2024).

24. Ibid.

25. Ronny Reyes, "Liberty Bell replica defaced with pro-Hamas symbols . . . during DC protest over Netanyahu's speech, *NY Post,* July 25, 2024, https://

nypost.com/2024/07/25/us-news/liberty-bell-replica-defaced-with-pro-hamas-symbols-by-anti-israel-protesters/ (accessed on July 25, 2024).

26. Ryan King and Alex Oliveira, "Anti-Israel rioters burn US flag, attempt to breach Capitol Police line as Netanyahu addresses Congress," NY Post, July 24, 2024, 6:30 p.m., https://nypost.com/2024/07/24/us-news/anti-israel-protesters-rip-down-burn-american-flag-in-dc-after-netanyahu-speech/ (accessed July 25, 2024).

27. TOI Staff and Emanuel Fabian, "'Massive tragedy': Children killed in Hezbollah rocket attack on soccer field are named," *The Times of Israel,* July 28, 2024, https://www.timesofisrael.com/massive-tragedy-kids-killed-in-hezbollah-rocket-attack-on-soccer-field-are-named/ (accessed on July 28, 2024).

3. Why Israel Matters Historically

1. Walter C. Kaiser, Jr., *A History of Israel: From the Bronze Age through the Jewish Wars,* (Nashville: B&H Academic, 2016), 3.

2. Ibid, 23.

3. Bryant G. Wood, "From Ramesses to Shiloh: Archaeological Discoveries Bearing on the Exodus-Judges Period," *Associates for Biblical Research,* https://biblearchaeology.org/research/chronological-categories/exodus-era/2403-from-ramesses-to-shiloh-archaeological-discoveries-bearing-on-the-exodusjudges-period/ (accessed July 28, 2024).

4. Bryan Windle, "Top Ten Discoveries Related to Abraham," *Bible Archaeology Report,* July 16, 2021, https://biblearchaeologyreport.com/2021/07/16/top-ten-discoveries-related-to-abraham/ (accessed July 27, 2024).

5. Avner Boskey, *Jews, Arabs, & the Middle East: A Messianic Perspective,* (Nashville: David's Tent Publishing, 2017), 63.

6. Ibid.

7. Bryan Windle, "Top Ten Discoveries Related to Abraham," *Bible Archaeology Report.*

8. G. Herbert Livingston, "The Archive of Mari," *Bible and Spade 5,* no. 4 (Fall 1992): 105–108.

9. Wikipedia contributors, "Cave of the Patriarchs," *Wikipedia, The Free Encyclopedia,* https://en.wikipedia.org/w/index.php?title=Cave_of_the_Patriarchs&oldid=1236391828 (accessed July 27, 2024).

10. See Gen 21:5.

11. Bryant G. Wood, "The Army of the Kings of Ur," *Associates for Biblical Research,* August 25, 2009, https://biblearchaeology.org/current-events-list/4045-the-army-of-the-kings-of-ur/ (accessed on July 20, 2024).

12. The periods and dates were gathered from the Associates for Biblical Research (ABR), which, as its website asserts, "is a Christian apologetics

ministry dedicated to demonstrating the historical reliability to the Bible through archaeological and biblical research." Their site is a treasure trove of information with blogs, articles, books, and videos. ABR Staff, "Associates for Biblical Research Statement on Ancient Near Eastern and Biblical Chronologies," *Associates for Biblical Research,* June 7, 2019, https://biblearchaeology.org/about/neareasternstatement/ (accessed on July 20, 2024).

13. Wikipedia contributors, "Merneptah Stele," *Wikipedia, The Free Encyclopedia,* https://en.wikipedia.org/w/index.php?title=Merneptah_Stele&oldid=1236305905 (accessed July 28, 2024).

14. "Discovery and Publication," *The Leon Levy Dead Sea Scrolls Digital Library,* https://www.deadseascrolls.org.il/learn-about-the-scrolls/discovery-and-publication/ (accessed on July 24, 2025).

15. BAS Staff, "The Tel Dan Inscription: The First Evidence of King David from the Bible," *Biblical Archeology Society,* June 4, 2024, https://www.biblicalarchaeology.org/daily/biblical-artifacts/the-tel-dan-inscription-the-first-historical-evidence-of-the-king-david-bible-story/ (accessed on July 15, 2024).

16. Bryan Windle, "Top Ten Discoveries in Biblical Archaeology in 2021," *Bible Archaeology Report,* https://biblearchaeologyreport.com/2021/12/28/top-ten-discoveries-in-biblical-archaeology-in-2021/ (accessed on July 27, 2024).

17. Avner Boskey, *Jews, Arabs, & the Middle East,* 160.

4. Why Israel Matters Politically

1. Reuters Fact Check, "Fact Check: ICC has requested, not issued arrest warrants for Netanyahu and Hamas Leaders," *Reuters,* May 21, 2024, https://www.reuters.com/fact-check/icc-has-requested-not-issued-arrest-warrants-netanyahu-hamas-leaders-2024-05-21/ (accessed July 29, 2024).

2. "From the River to the Sea," *American Jewish Committee,* https://www.ajc.org/translatehate/From-the-River-to-the-Sea/ (accessed on July 31, 2024).

3. Daniel Sokatch, *Can We Talk About Israel? A Guide for the Curious, Confused, and Conflicted,* (New York: Bloomsbury Publishing, 2022), 17.

4. Ibid.

5. Ibid.

6. Douglas J. Feith, "The Forgotten History of the Term 'Palestine,'" *Mosaic Magazine,* December 13, 2021, https://www.hudson.org/node/44363/ (accessed August 1, 2024).

7. Ibid.

8. Theodor Herzl, *A Jewish State: An Attempt at a Modern Solution of the Jewish Question,* (New York: Federation of American Zionists, 1917), ix.

9. Alan Dershowitz, *The Case for Israel,* (Nashville: Trade Paper Press, 2003), 6.
10. Ibid.
11. "Jewish & Non-Jewish Population of Israel/Palestine (1517–Present)," *Jewish Virtual Library,* https://www.jewishvirtuallibrary.org/jewish-and-non-jewish-population-of-israel-palestine-1517-present/ (accessed August 2, 2024).
12. Alan Dershowitz, *The Case for Israel,* 33.
13. Alan Dershowitz addresses the two-state solution in chapter 6 of his book *The Case for Israel* He states, "As soon as partition into two states or homelands was proposed, the Jews accepted it and the Arabs rejected it" (46).

5. Why Israel Matters Theologically

1. Referenced directly in Matt 22:44; Mark 12:36; Luke 20:42–43; Acts 2:33–34; Heb 1:13. Referenced indirectly in Matt 26:64; Luke 22:69; 1 Cor 15:25; Heb 5:6; 7:17, 21.
2. Rom 11:33.

6. Why Israel Matters to the Church

1. Rom 11:28.
2. Rom 11:25.
3. Isa 62:1.
4. Luke 18:3.
5. Luke 18:1.
6. Rom 9:3.

Top 20 Questions Answered

1. David Pawson, *Defending Christian Zionism,* (Travelers Rest, SC: True Potential, Inc., 2008), 9.
2. Wikipedia contributors, "Demographics of Israel," *Wikipedia,* https://en.wikipedia.org/wiki/Demographics_of_Israel/ (accessed August 11, 2024).
3. Ibid.

Glossary

1. This "working" definition was adopted on May 26, 2016 by the International Holocaust Remembrance Alliance (IHRA) Plenary in Bucharest. "Working definition of antisemitism," *International Holocaust Remembrance Alliance,* https://holocaustremembrance.com/resources/working-definition-antisemitism/ (accessed July 26, 2024).

2. Ibid.

3. Wikipedia contributors, "Arch of Titus," *Wikipedia, The Free Encyclopedia,* https://en.wikipedia.org/w/index.php?title=Arch_of_Titus&oldid=1232565661/ (accessed July 29, 2024).

4. "Ashkenazic and Sephardic Jews," *Judaism 101,* https://www.jewfaq.org/ashkenazic_and_sephardic/ (accessed July 25, 2024).

5. Lawrence Schiffman, "The Bar Kochba Revolt," *My Jewish Learning,* https://www.myjewishlearning.com/article/the-bar-kochba-revolt/ (accessed July 31, 2024).

6. Kali Robinson, "What Is Hamas?" Council on Foreign Relations, April 18, 2024, https://www.cfr.org/backgrounder/what-hamas/ (accessed July 24, 2024).

7. Kali Robinson, "What Is Hezbollah?" *Council on Foreign Relations,* https://www.cfr.org/backgrounder/what-hezbollah/ (accessed July 25, 2024).

8. Ibid.

9. "Introduction to the Holocaust," *US Holocaust Memorial Museum,* https://encyclopedia.ushmm.org/content/en/article/introduction-to-the-holocaust/ (accessed July 26, 2024).

10. Kali Robinson, "Iran's Support of the Houthis: What to Know," *Council on Foreign Relations,* March 1, 2024, https://www.cfr.org/in-brief/irans-support-houthis-what-know/ (accessed July 26, 2024).

11. American Jewish Committee, "What Does 'Globalize the Intifada' Mean and How Can it Lead to Targeting Jews with Violence?" *AJC/Global Voice,* December 4, 2023, https://www.ajc.org/news/what-does-globalize-the-intifada-mean-and-how-can-it-lead-to-targeting-jews-with-violence/ (accessed July 22, 2024).

12. "Europe 115: Kitos War," *Omniatlas,* https://omniatlas.com/maps/europe/1151014/ (accessed on July 30, 2024).

13. "Ashkenazic and Sephardic Jews," *Judaism 101.*

14. Douglas J. Feith, "The Forgotten History of the Term 'Palestine.'"

15. "Popular Front for the Liberation of Palestine (PFLP)," *Counter Terrorism Guide,* https://www.dni.gov/nctc/ftos/pflp_fto.html/ (accessed July 31, 2024).

16. "Ashkenazic and Sephardic Jews," *Judaism 101.*

17. See Article 1. Wikipedia contributors, "Montevideo Convention," *Wikipedia, The Free Encyclopedia,* https://en.wikipedia.org/w/index.php?title=Montevideo_Convention&o_did=1236780419/ (accessed July 28, 2024).
18. Richardson, *When a Jew Rules the World,* 13.
19. Daniel Gordis, *Israel,* 35.

ACKNOWLEDGMENTS

I'd like to once again thank Edie Mourey, my dear friend and coscribbler, without whom this book would not be a reality. The idea for putting out this little primer came just as both of us were entering into our summer vacations, and yet she put her heart and soul into bringing out the message that I had written and spoken over the last few years concerning Israel. I can't thank you enough, Edie.

Also, I'd like to thank my team at Radiant, led by some of the most dedicated and professional people who exist on the planet. Starting with Sean Downs, Cristin Riebel, Olivia Riddering Hayden, and Jeremy Shane, you guys are world class, and I can't thank you enough for helping me get this message out into the world at this tipping point in history.

Lastly, I'd like to acknowledge the one who is always by my side and championing me in every project, in every season. Jane, you are the wife of my youth, my best friend, and outside of Jesus, the greatest gift God has ever granted me. I am a man too blessed!

ABOUT THE AUTHOR

Lee Cummings is the founding pastor and senior leader of Radiant Church. Lee and his wife, Jane, started Radiant in 1996 in a high school auditorium in Richland, Michigan, a rural community in the outskirts of Kalamazoo. Since then, Radiant Church has grown to reach thousands of people in several locations. Radiant is a praying and worshiping church that is relentlessly leading people to become fully formed disciples of Jesus Christ living on mission together.

Since 2016, Lee has also served as the founder and overseer of the Radiant Network, a family of churches and leaders who share a common vision for growing the Kingdom.

Lee and Jane currently reside in Kalamazoo. They were married in 1992 and have three grown children, two sons-in-law, and three grandchildren.

ALSO BY LEE CUMMINGS

Take Heed, Watch & Pray: Overcoming Deception in the Last Days

Give No Rest! A Renewed Commitment to Pursue God's Presence in Prayer and Worship in the American Church

School of the Spirit: Living the Holy Spirit-Empowered Life

Be Radiant: Becoming Who God Meant You to Be

Flourish: Planting Your Life Where God Designed It to Thrive

SCAN FOR BOOKS, COURSES,
BLOGS, PODCASTS, AND MORE

@LEEMCUMMINGS